C O N T E M P O R A R Y ' S

FOUNDATIONS
READING

CONTEMPORARY'S
FOUNDATIONS
READING

JUDITH GALLAGHER

Project Editor
Cathy Niemet

NYSTL

Tewzer Eve

CB

CONTEMPORARY BOOKS

a division of NTC/CONTEMPORARY PUBLISHING GROUP
Lincolnwood, Illinois USA

Library of Congress Cataloging-in-Publication Data

Gallagher, Judith.
    Reading / Judith Gallagher.
        p.   cm. — (Contemporary's foundations)
    ISBN 0-8092-3833-0
    1. Reading comprehension—Handbooks, manuals, etc.   2. Life
skills—Handbooks, manuals, etc.   I. Title.   II. Series.
  LB1050.45.G35   1993
  428.4'071—dc20   92-39395
                                     CIP

ISBN: 0-8092-3833-0

Published by Contemporary Books,
a division of NTC/Contemporary Publishing Group, Inc.,
4255 West Touhy Avenue,
Lincolnwood (Chicago), Illinois 60646-1975 U.S.A.

8 9 0 DBH 9 8 7 6

Editorial Director
Caren Van Slyke

Assistant Editorial Director
Mark Boone

Editorial
Christine M. Benton

Editorial Assistant
Maggie McCann

Editorial Production Manager
Norma Fioretti

Production Editor
Thomas D. Scharf

Cover Design
Georgene Sainati

Illustrator
Cliff Hayes

Art & Production
Jan Geist
Sue Springston

Typography
Terrence Alan Stone

Cover photo © The Image Bank
Insert photograph by C. C. Cain Photography
Photo manipulation by Waselle Graphics

CONTENTS

Introduction 1

UNIT 1: PRACTICAL READING 2

Chapter 1: Finding the Main Idea 4

Exercise 1: How to Use Your Microwave Oven 6

Exercise 2: Keeping a Nontoxic House 8

Exercise 3: Juggling Daycare and a Job 10

Writing Workshop 11

Chapter 2: Finding Details 12

Exercise 1: USDA Revises Nutrition Guidelines 14

Exercise 2: The Shopping Mall Maze 16

Exercise 3: Looking for an Apartment 18

Writing Workshop 19

Chapter 3: Time Order 20

Exercise 1: Carrots with Ginger and Raisins 22

Exercise 2: How to Use an ATM 24

Exercise 3: Aerobic Exercise Session 26

Writing Workshop 27

Unit 1 Review: Giving Blood 28

UNIT 2: READING NONFICTION 30

Chapter 4: Main Idea and Reasons 32

Exercise 1: Biking Is Booming 34

Exercise 2: Who Should Decide What Kids Read? 36

Writing Workshop 37

Chapter 5: Facts and Opinions 38

Exercise 1: Two Views on Abortion 40

Exercise 2: A Review of *Exterminator 10* 42

Writing Workshop 43

Chapter 6: Detecting Bias 44

Exercise 1: Part A: Buy the Smooth Air Shoe! 46

Part B: Buy the Smooth Air Shoe! 47

Exercise 2: The Man with the Baboon Liver 48

Writing Workshop 49

Chapter 7: Making Inferences 50
Exercise 1: Margulies Cartoon 52
Exercise 2: Arlo & Janis Cartoon 54
Writing Workshop 55
Unit 2 Review: Secretarial Work Can Cause Stress 56

UNIT 3: READING POETRY 58
Chapter 8: Form 60
Exercise 1: "Well, Yes" 62
Exercise 2: "A Seeing Poem" 64
Writing Workshop 65

Chapter 9: Rhyme and Rhythm 66
Exercise 1: "The Veteran" 68
Exercise 2: "Love" 70
Writing Workshop 71

Chapter 10: Imagery 72
Exercise 1: "Beauty" 74
Exercise 2: "Swift Things Are Beautiful" 76
Writing Workshop 77

Chapter 11: Simile and Metaphor 78
Exercise 1: "Mother to Son" 80
Exercise 2: "Some People" 82
Writing Workshop 83
Unit 3 Review: "Joe" 84

UNIT 4: READING SHORT FICTION 86
Chapter 12: Character 88
Exercise: "The Eyes of Mr. Lovides" 90
Writing Workshop 95

Chapter 13: Setting 96
Exercise: "An American Twenty" 98
Writing Workshop 103

Chapter 14: Plot 104
Exercise: "The Wallet" 106
Writing Workshop 111

Chapter 15: Conflict 112

Exercise: "232-9979" 114

Writing Workshop 117

Chapter 16: Theme and Main Idea 118

Exercise: "Two Were Left" 120

Writing Workshop 123

Unit 4 Review: "Appalachian Home" 124

Post-Test 130

Post-Test Evaluation Chart 139

Post-Test Answer Key 140

Answer Key 141

ACKNOWLEDGMENTS

Photo on page 2 by Frank Siteman. Reprinted with permission of Stock Boston.

Food Pyramid Chart on page 14 copyright © 1992 by the *Washington Post*. Reprinted with permission.

Cartoon on page 15 by Jim Borgman. Reprinted with special permission of King Features Syndicate.

Photo on page 30 by Lisa A. Dellert. Reprinted with permission of the artist.

Photo on page 34 reprinted with permission of The Image Bank, Chicago.

Photo on page 40 reprinted with permission of UPI/Bettmann.

Photo on page 46 by Lisa A. Dellert. Reprinted with permission of the artist.

Photo on page 47 reprinted with permission of The Image Bank, Chicago.

Photo on page 48 reprinted with permission of AP/Wide World Photos.

Cartoon on page 51 by John Darkow. Reprinted with special permission of North America Syndicate.

Cartoon on page 52 by Jimmy Margulies, *The Record*/New Jersey. Copyright © 1992. Reprinted with permission of the artist.

Cartoon on page 54, "Arlo & Janis," copyright © 1992. Reprinted with permission of NEA, Inc.

Photo on page 58 reprinted with permission of AP/Wide World Photos.

Poem on page 60, "Fog," from *Chicago Poems*, by Carl Sandburg. Copyright © 1916 by Holt, Rinehart and Winston, Inc.; renewed 1944 by Carl Sandburg. Reprinted with permission of Harcourt Brace Jovanovich.

Poem on page 60, "Concrete Cat," by Dorothi Charles, from *An Introduction to Poetry*, seventh edition, by X. J. Kennedy. Copyright © 1990 by X. J. Kennedy. Reprinted with permission of HarperCollins Publishers.

Poem on page 62, "Well, Yes," from *Seeing Things*, by Robert Froman. Copyright © 1974 by Robert Froman. Published by Thomas Y. Crowell Company.

Poem on page 64, "A Seeing Poem," from *Street Poems*, by Robert Froman. Copyright © 1971 by Robert Froman. Published by Thomas Y. Crowell Company.

INTRODUCTION

Welcome to Contemporary's *Foundations: Reading.* With this book, you will build the reading and thinking skills you need to handle different types of reading materials successfully.

This book is divided into four units:

▶ **Practical Reading**, "survival" reading you do to function each day, such as reading recipes, instructions, or want ads

▶ **Nonfiction**, writing based on facts, which includes newspaper and magazine articles, commentaries, and book and movie reviews

▶ **Poetry**, verse that captures a person's feelings

▶ **Short Fiction**, stories created from an author's imagination

The reading skills you'll be learning with this book include finding the main idea, making inferences, finding cause and effect relationships, identifying facts and opinions, and detecting bias.

Foundations: Reading has special features that will help you build your reading, writing, and thinking skills. Keep your eye out for these:

Strategy boxes at the beginning of each chapter present a step-by-step guide for each new reading skill.

Pre-reading questions help you recall what you already know about a topic. They also pose some new questions to think about as you read a passage or look at an illustration.

A **Writing Workshop** at the end of each chapter gives you a chance to react to what you've read.

A **Post-Test** at the end of the book will help you see how well you've mastered the material in the book. The **Post-Test Answer Key** on page 140 will help you evaluate your answers. By filling out the **Post-Test Evaluation Chart** on page 139, you will see what skills you need to review.

We hope you enjoy the interesting topics in *Foundations: Reading.* We also invite you to explore the other books in Contemporary's *Foundations* series: *Social Studies, Science, Writing,* and *Mathematics.* We wish you the best of luck with your studies.

The Editors

UNIT 1
PRACTICAL READING

Practical reading is what you might call "survival" reading. It's the kind of reading you do every day to get the information you need to function well at work, at home, and in our society.

Newspapers provide good opportunities for practical reading. They can tell you everything from who is running for political office to what time your local theater is showing a movie you want to see. Practical reading material also includes recipes for cooking a new dish, instructions for programming a VCR, and clauses in the lease you sign when you rent an apartment.

PRACTICAL READING
TOPICS

- How to Handle Car Emergencies
- How to Use Your Microwave Oven
- Using Nontoxic Cleaning Products
- How to Juggle Daycare and a Job
- Advertising a Flea Market Sale
- New USDA Nutrition Guidelines
- Reading a Shopping Mall Map
- Reading an Ad for an Apartment
- How to Plant Tomatoes
- How to Make Carrots with Ginger and Raisins
- How to Use an ATM
- An Aerobic Exercise Session
- Giving Blood

AFTER READING THIS UNIT, YOU SHOULD BE ABLE TO
▶ FIND THE MAIN IDEA
▶ FIND DETAILS
▶ FOLLOW TIME ORDER IN INSTRUCTIONS

CHAPTER 1 | FINDING THE MAIN IDEA

You probably summarize main ideas every day. For example, you might watch a murder mystery on TV and then tell a friend about it the next day. You don't recite sixty minutes' worth of dialogue. You give a short version of the program. It includes only the main idea (who killed the victim?) and the important details (why? how?).

Newspaper reporters write about people and events that will interest their readers. When you read a newspaper or magazine, the headlines are probably the first thing you notice:

> **Crime Rate Increases**
> **Federal Reserve Lowers Interest Rates**
> **Air Pollution Controls Needed**
> **Chicago Bulls Win NBA Title Again**

A **headline** is a signal that announces the main idea of a news story or article. The **main idea** is a general statement that tells you the major point of an article.

Based on the headline, you can predict what the story will be about. You expect the story to give you more information about the headline. Notice how the following article explains the title—the main idea—more completely.

Drivers Should Plan Ahead for Car Emergencies

When a driving emergency happens, you won't have time to look up in a book what you should do. You have to react right away. You should plan ahead and study the steps to take in a driving emergency. Knowing the following facts could save your life.

First, if a tire blows out, do not step on the brakes. Steer the car as straight as possible as you apply gentle, even pressure to the brake pedal. Then pull slowly off the road. If you jam on the brakes, the car behind you may run into you.

Second, if the car skids on ice, steer in the direction of the skid. If the wheels go off the road onto a low shoulder, brake gently. Ride the shoulder until you can turn up onto the road. If you try to jerk the car back onto the road, you're likely to continue skidding.

Third, if your brakes fail, apply the parking brake slowly but firmly. If you have time, downshift the gears (from drive to second to first). You may even have time to shift into reverse, but *don't* shift into park. If downshifting doesn't bring the car to a halt, turn off the ignition. But don't turn the ignition to the lock position, because it locks the steering wheel in place. If all else fails, try to hit guardrails, fences, or signposts to slow the car.

You can avoid many emergencies in the first place by driving defensively. And always remember to buckle your seat belt, even if you're driving only a few blocks.

· ·

Let's look at how the article is organized. It has five paragraphs. The topic sentence states the main idea of a paragraph. The other sentences in the paragraph relate to the main idea. <u>A topic sentence often—but not always—begins a paragraph.</u>

■ Can you find the main idea of the first paragraph in the article? On the lines below, write the topic sentence:

What is the first paragraph's main idea about driving emergencies?

_____

_____

You were correct if you wrote the third sentence of the paragraph: **You should plan ahead and study the steps to take in a driving emergency.**

■ Go back and underline the topic sentence in each of the other paragraphs.

Did you underline the first sentence of each paragraph? If so, you found the correct topic sentences. All four paragraphs explain the main idea—Drivers Should Plan Ahead for Car Emergencies—in more detail.

STRATEGY: HOW TO FIND THE MAIN IDEA

▶ Read the entire story or article.
▶ Find the topic. *Whom* or *what* is the story or article about?
▶ What is the author's main point about the topic?
▶ Check to see if you have identified the correct main idea. Does each paragraph explain it in more detail?

Exercise 1

Read the instructions and complete the exercise that follows.

Good instructions start with the main idea and then give you steps to follow. Have you learned how to program a VCR or hook up a stereo? Did you think the instructions were easy to follow or not?

How to Use Your Microwave Oven

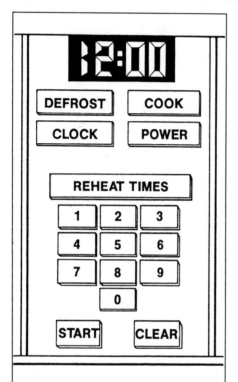

Before you use your new microwave oven, read the instructions carefully. Each oven has its own control panel, but most microwave ovens operate in a similar way. Look at the control panel shown here. It displays the time at the top of the panel. Under the time are the various functions. You can press *Defrost, Cook, Clock,* or *Power.* You can also warm food by pressing *Reheat Times.*

Under the functions are the numbers. These numbers are displayed as on a calculator, from zero through nine. You can press the numbers to set the cooking time in seconds or minutes. Under the numbers are *Start* and *Clear.*

A microwave oven will automatically cook on HIGH (power level 10) unless you enter a lower power level. Suppose you want to cook a serving of broccoli for two minutes and forty-five seconds on MEDIUM power (level 5). First, press the numbers *2, 4,* and *5* (two minutes, forty-five seconds). Then press *Power.* Next, press the number *5.* Finally, press *Start* to begin cooking. If you make a mistake, press *Clear.* This will clear the display and allow you to start over again.

Answer the questions in the space provided.

1. What is the main idea of the instructions?

   _____

2. What does the third paragraph tell you how to do?

   it tell you how can enter the time.

   _____

3. How would you cook green beans for two minutes and thirty seconds at power level 7?

   _____

   _____

4. What is the last function you press each time you set the controls?

   _____

5. What does pressing *Clear* allow you to do?

   _____

   Check your answers on page 141.

Exercise 2

Read the article and complete the exercise that follows.

Do you worry about pollution *inside* your house? What products do you use to clean your house? Do they ever make your eyes sting or your hands hurt?

Keeping a Nontoxic House

Many of the products you use to clean your house are probably **toxic**.[1] They can be made of powerful chemicals that can hurt you when you breathe them or touch them. Whether you're scrubbing a fiberglass bathtub or polishing wood furniture, most cleaners you buy at the store are stronger than they need to be. They can do more harm than good.

What steps can you take to avoid such indoor pollution? First, if you must use strong cleaners, wear rubber gloves. Then you won't absorb the chemicals through your skin. Second, make your own milder cleaning supplies. Third, read labels to identify which cleaners are dangerous. And fourth, look at some books that give earth-friendly housecleaning tips.

One good book on the subject is *Clean & Green* by Annie Berthold-Bond. It includes a recipe for a mild yet effective all-purpose cleaner. You can make it with everyday ingredients you buy at your local supermarket. Take a spray bottle and put in it 1 teaspoon of boric acid, ½ teaspoon of washing or sal soda, 2 tablespoons of vinegar or lemon juice, and ¼ teaspoon of liquid soap. Combine these

---

1toxic: poisonous

ingredients, then add 2 cups of very hot water. Shake the bottle gently until all the minerals dissolve. This solution will clean everything from vinyl floors to metal fixtures safely and thoroughly.

After you clean your house, make sure it is well ventilated, too. Vent your clothes dryer to the outdoors. Turn on a fan or open a window after showering to reduce indoor humidity. Use an exhaust fan when you cook. By taking all these steps, you will make your house nontoxic.

. . . .

Match each question with its answer.

_c_ **1.** What is the article about?

_e_ **2.** What is the third paragraph about?

_a_ **3.** What can you do to avoid contact with toxic agents?

_f_ **4.** How might dangerous chemicals get to you while you clean?

_d_ **5.** What are some things you can clean with the mixture in the spray bottle?

_b_ **6.** What is the topic of the second paragraph?

(a) wear rubber gloves, read labels, and read about earth-friendly cleaning

(b) how to avoid indoor pollution

(c) keeping a nontoxic house

(d) vinyl floors and metal fixtures

(e) a recipe for a safer cleaner

(f) They might be breathed in or absorbed through your skin.

Check your answers on page 141.

Exercise 3

Read the article and complete the exercise that follows.

Do you have children who go to daycare while you work? Do you think employers should help more with child care?

Juggling Daycare and a Job

If you have young children and work outside your home, you know how hard it is to juggle work schedules and daycare. You have to drop your children off for daycare and still get to work on time. This is how one family does it.

Rosa is a manager at an electronics firm. Her husband, Bob, works for a medical equipment company. They have a six-year-old daughter and a two-year-old son. They live in Washington, D.C. Every day, Bob drops their daughter off at a nearby grade school. Then he drives to his job, which is about thirty minutes away. Rosa takes their son downtown on the subway. She drops him off at a daycare center a few blocks from where she works.

Rosa and Bob both have to be flexible. If either parent has a late meeting or if either child has to see a doctor, they have to change their schedule. "When something comes up, we're back to square one," says Rosa. "Sometimes I think we'll be living from one crisis to the next until our son is 18."

Even though over 50 percent of mothers work outside their homes, society's and employers' policies have not caught up with this reality. A small number of employers now offer on-site daycare. Other employers pay for private daycare or offer job sharing for working parents. This means that two people share one full-time job. It makes it easier for both employees to work and to take care of their children. Companies are starting to realize that such programs make good business sense. Their workers are more productive. There is less absenteeism, tardiness, and staff turnover. And job satisfaction is increased when families find flexible work and can provide good daycare for their young children.

Circle the best answer for each question.

1. What is the main idea of the article?
   (1) Commuting to work is a hassle.
   (2) More and more mothers are working these days.
   (3) Employer-sponsored daycare is a bargain.
   (4) Juggling daycare and work schedules is hard to do.

2. How do Bob and Rosa manage their work and daycare schedules?

(1) Bob and Rosa work out of their home so that they don't have to juggle their work and daycare schedules.

(2) Bob drops off their daughter at school, while Rosa takes her son to daycare before she goes to work.

(3) Rosa drops off both children at a daycare center before she goes to work.

(4) Bob works at home and picks up the children from school and daycare at the end of each day.

3. What is the main idea of the last paragraph of the article?

(1) Some employers now offer on-site daycare programs.

(2) More mothers work outside the home than stay at home.

(3) Some employers offer job-sharing programs for working parents.

(4) Employers' and society's policies have not caught up with the fact that a majority of women work outside their homes.

4. What are some benefits to employers who provide child-care options?

(1) They make good business sense.

(2) They increase productivity and job satisfaction.

(3) They reduce absenteeism, tardiness, and staff turnover.

(4) all of the above

Check your answers on page 141.

WRITING WORKSHOP

Brainstorm: Find a Topic

Make a list of appliances and machines you know how to use. Review your list and choose one item to describe to someone.

Focus: Write a Topic Sentence

What is the purpose of the appliance or machine? Write a sentence stating the main idea. This is your topic sentence. Sample topic sentences are listed below.

▶ A chain saw can save you hours of work when cutting firewood.

▶ A VCR can let you watch TV programs that are on when you're not home.

Expand: Write a Paragraph

Develop your topic sentence into a paragraph. Add sentences that explain the topic sentence in more detail. Remember, every sentence of your paragraph should relate to the main idea stated in your topic sentence.

CHAPTER 2 | FINDING DETAILS

When news reporters write an article, they ask questions that begin with *who, what, where, when, why,* and *how.* The answers to these questions are often the **details** of a news story. As you learned in Chapter 1, details tell you more about the headline—the main idea.

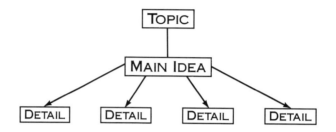

How can you use reporters' questions to improve your practical reading skills? As you read the poster below, ask yourself the questions: *who, what, where, when, why,* and *how.* Answering these questions will help you find the facts and information related to the main idea of the poster.

Flea Market Sale

Come one, come all, to the

FIRST ANNUAL CRABTREE FLEA MARKET!

It'll be the biggest sale you've seen all year. Great bargains on everything from china to picture frames to clothes to car tires. Prices start at 10¢. It's a sale you can't afford to miss!

- Sale items will be displayed at the Hi-Way Drive-in Theater, Route 30, 1 mile east of Crabtree.
- Saturday, June 20, from 9:00 A.M. until 9:00 P.M.
- Artists, farmers, and dealers from a 3-state area will be selling their treasures.
- China, glassware, art, furniture, lamps, plant stands, books, homemade jams and jellies, pictures and frames, clothing, towels, jewelry, tools, garden supplies, car parts, gently used TVs and stereos, audio- and videotapes, and more, more, MORE!

■ Based on the poster, answer the questions below.

1. What kinds of things will be on sale at the flea market?
   (1) clothes
   (2) furniture and lamps
   (3) car parts
   (4) all of the above

2. When will the flea market take place?
   (1) on Saturday, June 21, from 9:00 A.M. until 6:00 P.M.
   (2) on Saturday, May 3, from 10:00 A.M. until 8:00 P.M.
   (3) on Saturday, June 20, from 9:00 A.M. until 9:00 P.M.
   (4) on Saturday, March 20, from 8:00 A.M. until 7:00 P.M.

3. Where will the flea market take place?
   (1) at the Crabtree Theater on Route 25
   (2) at the Crafters Drive-in on Route 35
   (3) at the Hi-Way Drive-in Theater on Route 30
   (4) at the Market Street Theater in Crabtree

4. Who will sell goods at the flea market?
   (1) farmers from two nearby states
   (2) artists, farmers, and dealers from a 3-state area
   (3) dealers from the outlying suburbs
   (4) artists and photographers from the downtown area

Did you picture in your mind the details in the poster? For example, were you able to see the tables spilling over with china, glassware, and jewelry? Could you see rows of household items and furniture? The details paint a more complete picture of the main idea: the Crabtree Flea Market is a sale you won't want to miss.

Here are the answers: **1. (4)**, **2. (3)**, **3. (3)**, and **4. (2)**.

STRATEGY: HOW TO FIND DETAILS

▶ Ask the questions *Who? What? Where? When? Why?* and *How?*
▶ Picture in your mind what the author explains in the article.
▶ Check how the facts and information give you a clearer picture of the main idea.

Exercise 1

Read the passage and the Food Guide Pyramid.

How closely do your eating habits match those recommended in the new USDA food pyramid guidelines?

USDA Revises Nutrition Guidelines

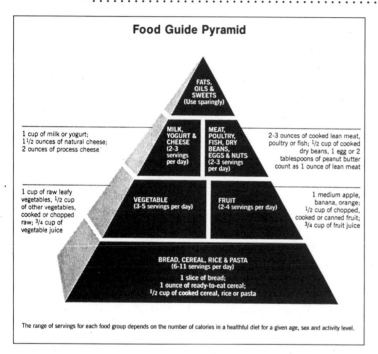

Food Guide Pyramid

FATS, OILS & SWEETS (Use sparingly)

1 cup of milk or yogurt; 1½ ounces of natural cheese; 2 ounces of process cheese

MILK, YOGURT & CHEESE (2-3 servings per day)

MEAT, POULTRY, FISH, DRY BEANS, EGGS & NUTS (2-3 servings per day)

2-3 ounces of cooked lean meat, poultry or fish; ½ cup of cooked dry beans, 1 egg or 2 tablespoons of peanut butter count as 1 ounce of lean meat

1 cup of raw leafy vegetables, ½ cup of other vegetables, cooked or chopped raw; ¾ cup of vegetable juice

VEGETABLE (3-5 servings per day)

FRUIT (2-4 servings per day)

1 medium apple, banana, orange; ½ cup of chopped, cooked or canned fruit; ¾ cup of fruit juice

BREAD, CEREAL, RICE & PASTA (6-11 servings per day)

1 slice of bread; 1 ounce of ready-to-eat cereal; ½ cup of cooked cereal, rice or pasta

The range of servings for each food group depends on the number of calories in a healthful diet for a given age, sex and activity level.

Do you want to know which foods are best for your health? Many people follow the U.S. Department of Agriculture (USDA) guidelines for healthy eating. The USDA has replaced its four basic food groups chart that stressed eating a variety of foods from each group. It now advises that some foods are better for you than others. It shows you which foods to eat more or less of in a pyramid-shaped chart.

Look first at the base of the pyramid. This is the grains group, which the USDA says should be the foundation of your diet. It recommends that you eat 6 to 11 servings a day from the grains group.

On the next level of the pyramid are the vegetable and fruit groups. The USDA advises that you eat 3 to 5 servings of vegetables and 2 to 4 servings of fruit a day.

On the next level are the dairy and protein groups. The USDA recommends that you consume 2 to 3 servings of milk, yogurt, or cheese a day. You should also eat 2 to 3 servings of meat, poultry, fish, dry beans, eggs, or nuts per day.

At the top of the pyramid is the fats, oils, and sweets group. This group includes fried foods, most "fast foods," and desserts made with sugar. The USDA says that you should eat foods in this group sparingly.

PART A

Answer the question in the space provided.

1. What is the purpose of the Food Guide?

_____

2. What food group should you eat the most of?

Fruit

3. How many servings of fruit should you eat each day?

3 - 5 servings fruit.

4. How much should you eat from the fats, oils, and sweets group?

So So

PART B

Read the cartoon. Then answer the questions.

"ACTUALLY, HARRY IS SOMETHING OF AN AUTHORITY ON THE FOOD PYRAMID HIMSELF......"

1. Which humorous detail shows the reader that the man is an authority on the food pyramid?

_____

2. Which detail in the kitchen shows the man's great interest in food?

_____

Check your answers on page 141.

Exercise 2

Read the passage and complete the exercise that follows.

Have you ever stopped at a gas station to ask directions and then been unable to follow them? Do you think that following a map is easier than following directions someone gives you?

The Shopping Mall Maze

Juan Rodríguez stopped at a new shopping mall last Saturday afternoon to buy a pair of black basketball shoes, size 9. The mall seemed enormous. In fact, it took him 15 minutes just to find a directory showing where the stores were located. The map looked like this:

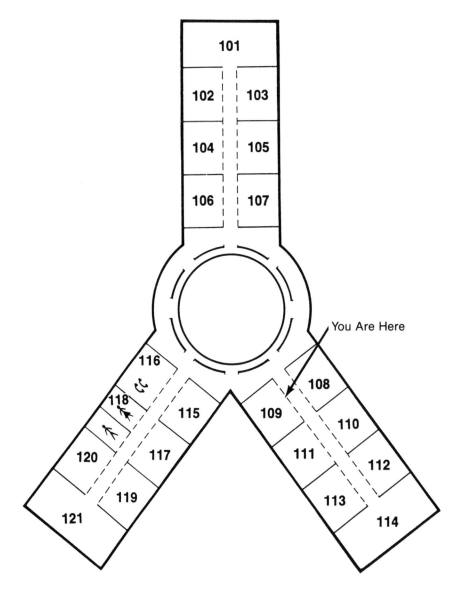

Directory

101 Troutman's Department Store	112 Handy Hardware
102 Klotz's Finer Shoes	113 The Piano Store
103 Toys, Toys, and More Toys	114 Blume's Department Store
104 Computer Wizard	115 Quality Sporting Goods
105 Generic Bookstore	116 public telephones
106 Hamburger Palace	117 Herbal Delights
107 Chocolate Dreams	118 public rest rooms
108 I Scream for Ice Cream	119 A World of Travel
109 Pizzarific	120 mall management office
110 Cosmetics R Us	121 Anything for a Dollar
111 Tiny Dancer Boutique	

The triangle on the map showed Juan that "you are here." There was a bank of public telephones next to the rest rooms, on the way to the store called Anything for a Dollar. Juan could tell from the symbols which was the men's rest room and which was the women's. And if he wanted to sit down, there were benches around the center of the mall. The key told Juan which store matched which number on the map.

· ·

Answer the questions in the space provided.

1. Between which two stores is Juan standing as he reads the map?

_____

2. How can Juan get to the toy store from where he is standing?

_____

3. How will Juan find the telephones once he has left the toy store?

_____

4. Juan's last stop is for pizza. How can he get there from the telephone area?

_____

Check your answers on page 141.

Exercise 3

Read the apartment ad.

Have you ever used the classified ads to look for an apartment, a job, a car, or a date? If so, you know how confusing abbreviations can be.

Looking for an Apartment

. . . .

This is a typical ad you might read about an apartment. Most of the words are abbreviated to save space.

> Spac. apt., Lake Pk. area. 3 br, 2 ba. Conv. loc. W/D, A/C, w/w cpt., fp, balc. Utls. incl., sec. dep. req. Call John at 555-3232 eves. Avail. Oct. 1.

. . . .

PART A
Match each abbreviation with the correct words.

____ **1.** br	**(a)**	washer/dryer
____ **2.** Utls incl.	**(b)**	convenient location
____ **3.** A/C	**(c)**	park
____ **4.** Conv. loc.	**(d)**	balcony
____ **5.** sec. dep. req.	**(e)**	wall-to-wall carpeting
____ **6.** Spac. apt.	**(f)**	utilities included
____ **7.** W/D	**(g)**	available
____ **8.** fp	**(h)**	security deposit required
____ **9.** balc.	**(i)**	fireplace
____ **10.** w/w cpt.	**(j)**	spacious apartment
____ **11.** ba.	**(k)**	bedrooms
____ **12.** avail.	**(l)**	October
____ **13.** Oct.	**(m)**	bathrooms
____ **14.** pk.	**(n)**	air conditioning

PART B

Match each question with the correct answer.

_____ **1.** Who is advertising the apartment?

_____ **2.** How many bedrooms does the apartment have?

_____ **3.** Where is the apartment located?

_____ **4.** When is the apartment available?

_____ **5.** What number should you call to ask about the apartment?

(a) 555-3232

(b) in the Lake Park area

(c) on October 1

(d) John

(e) 3

Check your answers on page 141.

WRITING WORKSHOP

Brainstorm: Think About Your Eating Habits

In this chapter, you read about the food pyramid that the USDA advises you to base your eating habits on. Diet is one of many important factors in maintaining good health. What kinds of food do you eat every day?

Gather facts and details about your eating habits. Ask yourself:
▶ Which foods do I eat for breakfast, lunch, and dinner every day?
▶ Which snack foods do I eat between meals?
▶ How many servings of food do I eat from each food group?
▶ When do I eat? when I'm hungry? worried? upset? bored?

Focus: Make a List of Facts

Write the answers to your questions. Then organize your answers into a list. Think of a title to describe your list.

Expand: Write a Paragraph

Write a topic sentence to begin a paragraph about your eating habits and how they affect your health. Then use your list of facts to write a paragraph about the details.

CHAPTER 3 | TIME ORDER

You can usually see a pattern of time order in the way things happen. For example: seven is the number *before* eight. Tuesday comes *after* Monday. *First,* you crawl. *Then,* you walk. *Next,* you learn to ride a bike. *Finally,* you learn to drive a car. Words like *before, after, first, then, next,* and *finally* are markers that show you time order.

The details, facts, and examples a writer uses to support the main idea are placed in a paragraph in a certain order. Usually it's the order in which events happened, or **time order**. Knowing that an article uses this pattern can make it easier for you to read. You can look for dates and times that show when things happened.

A history book is a good example of writing in chronological, or time, order. So is a biography, a story of someone's life. A biography usually starts when the person is born and continues in time order until his or her death. How-to instructions and recipes almost always follow time order to make it easier for you to follow them.

The following article tells you how to plant tomatoes. As you read, picture in your mind the steps it describes.

Time to Plant Tomatoes

To grow your own tomatoes, you must first buy tomato plants when the weather is warm. This might be in May, depending on where you live. Then, water the tomatoes before you pull them out of their pots.

Next, dig a shallow but wide hole in the ground. Then, put the tomato plants in the dirt at a slant. The root system should be only four inches below the surface, where the soil temperature is still warm. But all of the stem except the top couple of inches should be buried so the plant can develop strong roots.

Next, after the plants begin to produce fruit, sprinkle some fertilizer in a circle around each stem. Then, water the plants well. Next, in about a month, put at least three inches of mulch around each plant. Finally, surround the plants with wire cages. This will give the stems support as they start to climb. Before you know it, you will be eating juicy, red tomatoes from your own healthy plants.

■ First, look for the time order words in the directions on page 20. Then, make a list of the steps you would take to grow tomatoes.

1. _____   5. _____

2. _____   6. _____

3. _____   7. _____

4. _____   8. _____

Finally, if your list looks like the one shown, you understand time order.

1. **Buy tomato plants.**

2. **Water them.**

3. **Dig a hole in the ground.**

4. **Plant each tomato at a slant.**

5. **Add fertilizer.**

6. **Water the plants.**

7. **Mulch the plants.**

8. **Put up wire cages around the plants.**

STRATEGY: HOW TO FOLLOW TIME ORDER

▶ Read the entire article or set of directions.
▶ Look for words like *before*, *after*, *first*, *then*, *next*, and *finally*.
▶ Picture in your mind the events or steps described.

Exercise 1

Read the recipe and complete the exercise that follows.

Have you ever tried to follow a new recipe and flopped? Following the wrong time order may have been the problem, even in a simple meal.

Carrots with Ginger and Raisins

Ingredients:

6 fresh carrots

2 tablespoons butter

1 teaspoon sugar

2 teaspoons chopped gingerroot

1 cup chicken broth

2 tablespoons golden raisins

2 teaspoons chopped parsley

Clean, trim, and peel the carrots. Cut them into slices ½-inch thick. Then put the carrots, butter, sugar, gingerroot, and chicken broth in a saucepan. Simmer them, covered, for 20 minutes. Then stir in the raisins. Cook, uncovered, for 5 more minutes. Toss the carrots with parsley. Serves 4.

Write the 7 steps in correct time order.

1. _____

2. _____

3. _____
   _____

4. _____
   _____

5. _____
   _____

6. _____
   _____

7. _____
   _____

Check your answers on pages 141-142.

Exercise 2

Read the article and complete the exercise that follows.

Do you have an automated teller machine (ATM) card with your bank? If so, do you prefer doing business through the machine or with a live teller? Do you use the ATM when the bank is closed?

How to Use an ATM

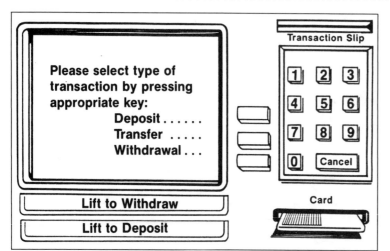

Pat Brown went to her bank to get an ATM card. It is a small plastic rectangle that looks like a credit card. A few weeks later, the bank mailed her a card and her four-digit personal identification number (PIN). Her PIN is 1234.

As Pat was getting ready for bed one night, she realized that she had only $2 in her wallet. She had to give $10 for a going-away lunch for a co-worker the next day. She didn't want to get up early to go to the bank. So she decided to go to the bank that night. She used her ATM card to withdraw $50 from her checking account.

These are the steps she followed to withdraw money. First, she put her card in the lower slot on the right side of the machine. She made sure her card was facing the right way. Second, the computer screen said, "Please enter your PIN." Pat pressed the numbers *1, 2, 3,* and *4.* Next, the screen said, "Please select type of transaction by pressing appropriate key." Pat pressed the bottom key for *Withdrawal.*

Then the screen said, "From which account?" The choices it gave were *Checking, Savings,* and *Money market.* Pat pressed the key for *Checking.* Next, the screen said, "Please select amount of transaction in multiples of ten." Pat pushed the number *5* and then *0* three times, until the screen read, "50.00." The screen then read, "Please wait." In less than a minute, it read, "Please lift the lid and remove your withdrawal."

Pat lifted the lid marked *Withdraw.* She counted her $50 to make sure the ATM didn't make a mistake. Then she waited for her withdrawal slip to come out of the slot at the upper right corner of the machine. Pat checked the slip to make sure it was correct. Then her ATM card was returned through the card slot. She put it in her wallet and walked away. If Pat had made a mistake at any point by pressing the wrong button, she could have pressed *Cancel* and started over again.

....

Circle the best answer for each question.

1. What was Pat's first step?
   (1) pressing the withdrawal button
   (2) inserting her ATM card
   (3) counting her money
   (4) getting her withdrawal slip

2. What did Pat do immediately after selecting the account?
   (1) selected whether to withdraw, deposit, or transfer money
   (2) lifted the lid and removed her money
   (3) selected the amount of money she wanted to withdraw
   (4) removed her ATM card

3. When did Pat enter her PIN?
   (1) right after inserting her card
   (2) right before selecting the account
   (3) right before selecting the amount of money
   (4) right after selecting withdrawal

4. When did Pat select the type of transaction?
   (1) right after selecting which account she wants
   (2) right before receiving her withdrawal slip
   (3) right before selecting the amount
   (4) right after recording her PIN

5. What did Pat do when the screen said, "Please lift the lid . . . ?"
   (1) retrieved her card
   (2) removed her $50
   (3) selected the type of transaction she wanted
   (4) picked up her withdrawal slip

Check your answers on page 142.

Exercise 3

Read the article and complete the exercise that follows.

Do you follow an exercise program? If so, does it include the same warm-up and cool-down phases as the following program?

Aerobic Exercise Session

· ·

First, get your doctor's permission to start an aerobic exercise program. He or she will check your general physical condition and tell you whether it's safe to start exercising.

Make sure each session starts with a warm-up period. You should stretch your muscles and get them ready for your workout. Warm up for at least five minutes.

Then start the actual training session. Jog, bike, or do exercises that get your heart rate up to the target range. Depending on your age and your physical condition, aim to raise your pulse rate to between 140 and 160 beats per minute. Take your pulse during exercise to make sure your heart rate doesn't get too fast.

Pulse Rate	Resting Rate	Warm-Up Period 5 minutes	Aerobic Exercise 20 minutes	Cool-Down Period 5 minutes	Recovery Period
160 150 140 130 120 110 100 90 80 70					

After the 20-minute aerobic session, start cooling down. Do a few gentle stretches while you catch your breath. If your heart rate does not return to a resting rate (about 70) within five minutes, you're working out too hard. Finally, during the recovery period, sit down and relax.

· ·

Answer the questions in the space provided.

1. How long should the aerobic exercise part of the session last?

_____

2. What comes right after the aerobic exercise?

_____

3. What should your pulse rate be at the beginning of the cool-down phase?

_____

4. What is the maximum safe pulse rate at any time?

_____

5. How long should the warm-up phase last?

_____

6. What does the graph show as a typical resting pulse rate?

_____

Check your answers on page 142.

WRITING WORKSHOP

Brainstorm: Make a List of Steps

You just read about how to plant tomatoes, how to follow a recipe for carrots with ginger and raisins, how to use an ATM, and how to do aerobic exercises. Choose a recipe or an activity that has several steps you must follow in order. Make a list of these steps.

Focus: Put Steps in Time Order

Review your list. Put the steps in logical order so that they are easy for someone else to follow.

Expand: Write a Summary

Write a paragraph that summarizes the steps needed to follow your set of directions. Ask a friend or co-worker to check your set of directions.

UNIT 1
REVIEW

Read the article and complete the exercise that follows.

Have you ever donated blood? Have you, or a member of your family, ever needed blood after an accident or an illness?

Giving Blood

Donating blood is a safe, easy process that can save someone's life. You can be the source of blood needed to treat people with injuries and illnesses such as cancer, anemia, and **hemophilia**.[1] Blood is needed constantly, year-round.

Your single donation may help three or more patients, because your whole blood is broken down into its parts. Each part can then be used to treat a different person for a different disease. For example, red blood cells are used to treat anemia and make routine blood transfusions. **Platelets**[2] are used mainly for cancer patients. Fresh frozen plasma (the liquid part of the blood) is used to treat shock and clotting problems.

To give blood, you must be at least 17, weigh at least 110 pounds, and be in good health. It is safe to donate as often as every two months. That's more than enough time for your body to rebuild its supply. Everyone is a potential blood recipient (one who receives blood). But only about half of us meet the age and medical requirements to be donors (who give blood). That's why it's so important for everyone who can give blood to do so.

It is impossible for a donor to get AIDS—or any other illness—from donating blood if correct procedures are used. The blood technician uses a new, sterile needle for each person who gives blood. The needle is used only once and then destroyed. So it can't carry an infection to the next donor.

You can give blood for a specific friend or family member who is going to have surgery. If you're scheduled for an operation, you can also give blood for yourself ahead of time. That way you can entirely eliminate the small chance of being infected by receiving someone else's blood. All blood is screened for signs of infection before it's used. These tests are nearly 100 percent accurate. The risk of refusing a needed transfusion is far greater than the risk of infection.

---

[1] **hemophilia:** an inherited blood defect found in males, marked by delayed clotting of blood

[2] **platelets:** small disks in the blood of vertebrate animals that assist in blood clotting

It takes only an hour to give the gift of life. First, your temperature, pulse, blood pressure, and hemoglobin (iron) levels are checked. Your health history is reviewed. Then, the nurse withdraws your blood. This process takes less than ten minutes. You'll give less than a pint, or one-twelfth of your blood supply.

Afterward, you'll be served fruit juice to help your body rebuild its blood supply. It rebuilds plasma in just a few hours and blood cells within a few weeks. All blood types are needed, and the process is quick and easy.

....

Circle the best answer for each question.

1. What is the main idea of the first paragraph?
   (1) Blood is needed constantly.
   (2) Anemia is the main reason for blood transfusions.
   (3) Donating blood is safe and easy and can save a life.
   (4) You can be the source of needed blood.

2. The blood you donate can be
   (1) broken down into parts for as many as three patients
   (2) given whole to cancer patients
   (3) used only by shock victims
   (4) refrigerated for at least a year

3. You can't give blood if you
   (1) are under 17 years old
   (2) weigh less than 110 pounds
   (3) have AIDS
   (4) all of the above

4. It is impossible to get AIDS from donating blood if correct procedures are used because
   (1) needles are used more than once
   (2) new, clean needles are used for each person
   (3) needles don't carry infection
   (4) needles are shared by family members only

5. When you give blood,
   (1) about a quart of liquid is removed from your body
   (2) you are asked for your health history
   (3) you can't eat or drink anything for three hours
   (4) you'll feel weak for about a month

Check your answers on page 142.

UNIT 2
READING NONFICTION

Nonfiction includes many types of material. Among them are newspaper reports, magazine articles, instructions, and books on everything from history to biography to gardening. Good reading skills come in handy both at work and in your free time. They can help you get a good job or to learn new tasks.

To get the most out of what you read, it is not enough just to recognize the words. You should also be able to understand what you read and think about the writer's purpose. That purpose may be to inform, persuade, or entertain you. You bring your life experience, stored knowledge, and a common language to what you read. This background helps you understand more completely what the writer is trying to say. Sometimes, writers spell out their point in detail. Other times, they imply their meaning indirectly.

NONFICTION

TOPICS

- Cultures Clash About an Observatory Site
- The Popularity of Biking
- Who Should Decide What Kids Read?
- Two Views on the Los Angeles Riots
- Pro-Choice and Anti-Abortion Issues
- A Movie Review of *Exterminator 10*
- A Biased Campaign Speech
- Reading Product Ads
- Animal Rights Issues
- Campaign Commercial: Parental Guidance Suggested
- The Plight of the Homeless
- Equal Pay?
- The Stresses Facing Secretaries

AFTER READING THIS UNIT, YOU SHOULD BE ABLE TO
▶ FIND THE MAIN IDEA AND REASONS
▶ TELL THE DIFFERENCE BETWEEN FACTS AND OPINIONS
▶ RECOGNIZE BIAS AND POINT OF VIEW
▶ MAKE INFERENCES FROM WHAT YOU READ

CHAPTER 4 | MAIN IDEA AND REASONS

A writer often gives several reasons to support a main idea. For example, read the next sentence.

Sue started looking for a new job because her work was boring, it didn't pay enough, and her boss was a bully.

■ How many reasons does the writer give for the main idea—Sue's decision to look for a new job? _____

Did you write *three*? The reasons are: **(1) her work was boring, (2) it didn't pay enough, and (3) her boss was a bully.**

Notice how the following article is organized. It tells you how two sides disagree about the main idea—whether to build a telescope in Arizona.

Religions Clash on Arizona Mountaintop

It's the Apache Indian tribes vs. the Catholic Church. They disagree about the proper use of a piece of land in southeastern Arizona. The church's Vatican Observatory is part of a group that wants to build Mount Graham International Observatory at the site. The group chose Mount Graham because the mountain is 10,700 feet high. Also, the skies above it are not polluted. This means scientists could see the stars clearly from the mountaintop. The $200 million construction project has already begun. The builders plan to install telescopes across a nine-acre section of mountaintop. They will use the telescopes to study the stars.

The Apaches are trying to stop the building because the mountain contains their ancestors' burial sites. They see the bulldozers and cement trucks tearing into the ground. And they see their holy land being destroyed forever.

Franklin Stanley, an Apache spiritual leader, says, "The gods speak to us from the mountain. We worship on the mountain. I am not saying that the waters, the plants, or the mountain *is* our god, as in pagan idol worship. Our idea of a god is closer to what Christians would recognize, since Catholics, for instance, have holy water, saints who have healing powers, believe in visions, and have sacred sites where respect is essential."

Catholics also have the Reverend George Coyne, director of the Vatican Observatory. Coyne is a Jesuit priest with a doctoral degree in astronomy. He is one of the main supporters of building the observatory. He says environmental groups like the Audubon Society and Earth First are trying to use the Apaches in their own interests. But the Apaches say there are other locations that would make good observatories. Those other locations are not sacred sites for them.

Mount Graham was taken from the Apaches by the U.S. government in 1874. It's now part of the Coronado National Forest. The Apaches have sued the observatory because they believe building the observatory is illegal. They say it breaks the American Indian Religious Act, the Historic Preservation Act, and other laws. "If you take Mount Graham from us, you will take our culture," says Stanley. "Why do you try to take my church away and treat the mountain as if it was about money instead of respect?"

. . . .

Let's look at how the story is organized. It has five paragraphs. Paragraph 1 explains why the Vatican wants to build the observatory. Paragraphs 2 and 5 explain why the Apaches don't want it to be built. The quote in paragraph 3 gives more details about the Apaches' reasons. Paragraph 4 gives another reason for each side.

■ List one reason given in the passage for the Apaches' position. The Apaches want to stop the Mount Graham project because

---

You were correct if you wrote any of the following: **Mount Graham is the Apaches' burial ground and holy land. There are other sites where an observatory could be built. The project is illegal and would break several laws.**

■ Now go back and underline the reasons why the Vatican wants to build on Mount Graham. Did you underline these reasons? **The group chose Mount Graham because the mountain is 10,700 feet high. Also, the skies there are clear and unpolluted. This means scientists could see the stars clearly from the mountaintop.**

STRATEGY: HOW TO FIND OUT WHY
▶ Read the entire article.
▶ Find the topic. What is the author's main point?
▶ Check for words like *because, since, therefore, due to,* and *consequently.* Are they followed by reasons why the main point happened?
▶ List the reasons given in the article. Do they help you understand the main idea better?

Exercise 1

Read the article and complete the exercise that follows.

How do you get to work every day? Do you ever get frustrated by your method of travel and wish there were some other way to go? Would you be able to bike to your job?

Biking Is Booming

Bicycling is becoming more and more popular in the United States. It's both a sport and a way to commute to work. According to the Bicycle Institute of America, more than 3.5 million people rode their bikes to work in 1991. Ten years ago, only 1.5 million did. Counting biking for fun, more than 80 million Americans ride these days.

Biking has become popular for many reasons. Physical fitness is perhaps the most important. "I don't have to spend an hour in the gym when I get home," says accountant Amy Packard. "I live eight miles from my job. So I get my workout by biking to and from the office."

Biking can actually be faster than driving or using public transportation. In the bike lane, Mark Simpson zips past cars in traffic jams to his job in Palo Alto, California. Riding a bike is cheaper than paying train or bus fare. It's also cheaper than paying for gas and city parking. People who are concerned about the environment like bicycles because they don't pollute. In fact, some companies give away bikes to employees who promise to use them to get to work.

The safety record of bikers is also improving. The government's traffic agency says this is probably due to increased use of helmets and better training of cyclists. Biking is also a great way for families to have fun together. And everyone gets a good workout. They also get fresh air and the pleasure of time spent with loved ones.

There are some drawbacks to biking. The biggest one is probably bad weather. Even bike fanatics tend to stay off their wheels during the coldest, iciest months. Traffic can also be a problem. There are not enough bike paths and bike lanes on roads. For commuters, finding a safe place to park their bikes is hard.

But Congress is considering a bill to encourage biking. If it passes, the Bicycle and **Pedestrian**[1] Improvement Act will allot more than $100 million a year. The money will go to build bike racks and bike and pedestrian paths.

....

Circle the best answer for each question.

1. What is the topic of the whole article?
  (1) Highways are too crowded.
  (2) Bicycling is getting more popular.
  (3) Riding the bus is expensive.
  (4) You have to be a fitness nut to ride a bike.

2. What is one reason given for the boom in biking?
  (1) It's good for the rider and for the environment.
  (2) It's easy even in winter and heavy traffic.
  (3) Parking for bikes is cheap and plentiful in most cities.
  (4) Bikes are more comfortable than cars.

3. What is listed as a drawback of biking?
  (1) fresh air
  (2) overdeveloped muscles
  (3) takes too long
  (4) not enough bike paths

4. Why is the safety record of bikes improving?
  (1) Smarter people are riding them.
  (2) They're built with advanced technology.
  (3) More riders are using helmets.
  (4) Global warming has cut down on icy weather.

5. Why do fewer people bicycle in the winter?
  (1) The weather is too cold and icy.
  (2) They're too busy watching first-run TV shows.
  (3) That's when they take vacations.
  (4) They prefer to walk then.

Check your answers on page 142.

---

¹pedestrian: one who goes on foot

Exercise 2

Read the passage and complete the exercise that follows.

Should public libraries keep certain kinds of books off the shelves?

Who Should Decide What Kids Read?

Should public schools and public libraries be in the book-banning business? Free libraries were started in this country to give people uncensored access to information. (Censorship is the practice of controlling what people are allowed to read.) The idea was that if citizens were exposed to all kinds of ideas, they could make up their own minds about what to think. In a democracy, the better informed people are, the better able they are to make good decisions.

In recent years, some parents and religious groups don't want their children to read the classic novel *The Catcher in the Rye* because the main character swears. Others want to ban *The Diary of a Young Girl*, the true story of Anne Frank, who was killed by the Nazis in World War II, because of its sexual overtones.

Some want to ban *Huckleberry Finn* because they say it's racist. Actually, this novel presents a strong argument against racism. Others want to ban *Free to Be You and Me* because it talks about women doing jobs that require physical strength and men doing housework.

One woman sued her local school board. She wanted it to ban the book *Dragonwings* by Laurence Yep. It's the story of a Chinese boy who moves to San Francisco in the early 1900s. The book describes his struggles to fit into his new environment. Many Chinese immigrants at that time used the word *demons* to refer to white people. The woman who wants to ban the book is offended by that word and by the book's discussion of magical beings.

Dragonwings has won several awards for quality. School officials say it helps readers understand other cultures. The school board excused the woman's son from reading the book. But she wants the board to stop other children from reading it, too. She thinks it will be a bad influence on children.

Should a whole school district miss out on an award-winning book because one parent doesn't like it? Should teachers and librarians protect children from profanity? Should children be shielded from reading about the Nazi movement, racism, and sexism? Or is learning about harsh realities the best way to learn how to deal with them? There are no easy answers.

Answer the questions in the space provided.

1. Why did early libraries not censor books?

_____

2. Why do some people want to ban *Huckleberry Finn*?

_____

3. Why does one parent want to ban *Dragonwings*?

_____

4. Why did the school board refuse to ban *Dragonwings*?

_____

Check your answers on page 142.

WRITING WORKSHOP

Brainstorm: Find a Topic

Think about the sports or hobbies you enjoy. Make a list of them. Choose one item to describe to someone.

Focus: Write Your Reasons Why

Why do you enjoy the activity? You probably have several reasons. Sample reasons are listed below.

▶ I like to paint with watercolors because it's challenging. It's hard to get both the shapes and the colors exactly right, such as a sailboat on a lake.

▶ I like to watch pro basketball because it's faster, higher-scoring, and more exciting than other winter sports.

Expand: Write a Paragraph

Develop your description of your activity into a paragraph. Make sure you include the reasons why you enjoy it. Imagine that you're trying to persuade someone who doesn't like your hobby that it would be fun to try.

CHAPTER 5 | FACTS AND OPINIONS

To fully understand the nonfiction that you read, you have to understand the difference between facts and opinions. A **fact** can be proved by gathering information to support it. An **opinion** cannot be proved. An opinion often has a phrase like *I think, I feel,* or *I believe.*

You can't believe everything you read. Letters to the editor, commentaries and essays, and reviews of books and movies are all written to persuade their readers about their opinions.

■ Read each of the statements. Are they *facts* or *opinions?*

(1) American workers aren't smart enough to compete with the Japanese.
(2) Americans buy more goods from Japan than the Japanese do from the United States.
(3) I think that the American society is healthier than the Japanese because the U.S. society allows creativity.

Only the second statement is a fact. You could prove it by finding out how much money each country spends to buy the other country's goods. The first and third statements are opinions. It's impossible to gather information to measure the intelligence of a large group of people. It's equally impossible to measure the health of a society based on its freedom to create. So the third statement cannot be proved true or false.

People who write letters to the editor in newspapers and magazines may be more interested in convincing others to think as they do than in sticking to the facts. For example, read the following letters on the emotionally charged subject of the 1992 riots in Los Angeles.

Two Views on the L.A. Riots

Your story on the L.A. riots suggested they were caused by an all-white jury. Sure, the jury found four white police officers not guilty of beating black motorist Rodney King. Did they light the matches that burned down small businesses in Los Angeles? Then how can it be their fault? The people who caused the riots are the ones who were burning, looting, and smashing windows. In my opinion, they have only themselves to blame. President Bush said our justice system works. I think that means the jury was right.

—Bud Snyder, Simi Valley, California

I say to Bud Snyder—wake up and smell the coffee! The jury that didn't punish the white police officers did indeed light the match, in a sense. The fuel was racism. I think it's racism that keeps so many of my friends and neighbors poor and unemployed. Some of the people you called looters were mothers taking home food for their starving babies. Others just gave up on the system when they heard the **verdict**.[1] That jury saw the same tape we did. It showed the cops beating Rodney King unconscious. They still decided the cops were innocent. For years, when blacks complained about racist attacks, whites told us to prove it. Now someone did, with a video camera. I can't believe whites have still managed to ignore it.

—Kim Richards, Detroit, Michigan

Both letter writers read the same article. They both saw the videotape of the King beating and TV coverage of the riots. But they had very different reactions to it. Each chose the facts that would make his or her opinion sound right.

■ Read the following four statements. Which are facts and which are opinions?

▶ I think it's racism that keeps so many of my friends and neighbors poor and unemployed.

▶ That jury saw the same tape we did.

▶ It [the tape] showed the cops beating Rodney King unconscious.

▶ I think that means the jury was right.

Did you identify the first and last statements as opinions? (Both statements also began with the words *I think*.) **Did you identify the second and third statements as facts that can be proved?**

STRATEGY: HOW TO TELL FACTS FROM OPINIONS

▶ For each statement, ask, "Can this be proved true or false?"

▶ Watch for phrases like *in my opinion, I think, I feel*, and *should be*. They signal that an opinion is being stated.

▶ Look for emotionally loaded words like *terrible, crazy, fantastic*, and *wonderful*, which are used to express opinions.

---

[1]**verdict:** the decision reached by a jury

Exercise 1

Read the passages and complete the exercise that follows.

Commentaries are often slanted to reflect the authors' opinions. Papers often publish essays on the same subject by people with different viewpoints. When you read both sides, you get more of the whole story.

Two Views on Abortion

PRO-CHOICE IS NO CHOICE

A lot of people talk about the freedom of choice. But pro-choice is no choice because it says killing babies is legal. It violates the Golden Rule.

In 1972, the U.S. Supreme Court ruled in *Roe v. Wade* that abortion was legal in this country. Finally, 20 years and thousands of lost lives later, the court has taken a step to end that evil. It upheld the Pennsylvania abortion law, which makes abortions harder to get.

But that's only the first step. Babies across this great land are still dying. We have to outlaw all abortions in every state and stop shedding innocent blood.

Pro-choicers argue that a fetus is not a human life. But doctors have seen many seven-month-old fetuses survive on their own. Abortionists perform the operation in the first three months after conception. If we let them get away with that, they'll start killing babies after they're born.

—Miriam Galt

THE LAST PLACE GOVERNMENT BELONGS

Women will never have equality until they have control over their own bodies. A big part of that control is the right to choose whether and when to have children. The government should not have the right to tell a husband and wife how to run their family.

Recently, the U.S. Supreme Court gave the government that power. It did so by upholding the Pennsylvania abortion law. The law requires parental consent, counseling, and waiting periods. These can all cause financial and emotional hardship. This petty law treats women like children.

Can the government insist that a woman carry a deformed baby to term? Can it make a pregnant 15-year-old go through nine months of pregnancy and then labor? Childbirth can be fatal for someone so young. Can it insist that a rape victim have her rapist's baby? According to the Pennsylvania law, it can.

The state pretends to have resolved all moral questions about abortion. But all it has really done is impose the values of antichoice fanatics, a minority group, on all of its people. Government has now intruded into the most private area of family life. It's the last place government belongs.

—Tanya Taft

. . . .

Circle *F* for a fact or *O* for an opinion.

F   O   **1.** But pro-choice is no choice because it says killing babies is legal.

F   O   **2.** It [abortion] violates the Golden Rule.

F   O   **3.** In 1972, the U.S. Supreme Court ruled in *Roe* v. *Wade* that abortion was legal in this country.

F   O   **4.** Twenty years after *Roe* v. *Wade*, the court upheld the Pennsylvania abortion law.

F   O   **5.** But doctors have seen many seven-month fetuses survive on their own.

F   O   **6.** It's [Abortion is] the last place government belongs.

F   O   **7.** Women should carry deformed babies to full term.

F   O   **8.** The [Pennsylvania] law requires parental consent, counseling, and waiting periods.

F   O   **9.** This petty law treats women like children.

F   O   **10.** The government should control the most private area of family life.

Check your answers on page 142.

Exercise 2

Read the passage and complete the exercise that follows.

Do you tell your friends about a good book or a movie so they can enjoy it, too? A reviewer's job is to describe a work well enough so that you have some idea whether you want to spend your time and money on it.

A Review of *Exterminator 10*

The latest entry in the violent series of *Exterminator* movies lives up to its name. If you think the higher the body count, the better the movie, this one's for you. At least two dozen people die in the first hour, in clever and disgusting ways.

Newcomer Lance Cooper stars as Mack Starr, the undercover agent who makes his own rules. In *Exterminator 10*, he slashes through the jungles of South America. He is looking for the leaders of a drug-smuggling ring. You'd think after ten movies you'd know a lot about a character. You'd have seen him grow and change and care about what happens to him. But Mack Starr never changes. He's always been a cardboard spy, a sort of third-rate James Bond.

Will Starr find the evil drug dealers? Will he devise new ways to destroy them? Will he get out alive? Let's put it this way: *Exterminator 11* is already scheduled to come out next summer. It'll be just in time for the drive-in circuit.

For many fans, the highlight of this movie will be the special effects. I must admit that they are amazing. Bullet holes and gaping wounds, fake shotgun blasts, and severed limbs are shown in a most convincing fashion. Even the blood looks real. And the scene where the lab blows up rivals any fireworks display.

The one other good thing I can say for this movie is that character actor Joe Bara does a nice job as the bad guy. He seems almost human. In contrast, the rest of the cast are basically sleepwalking. If you like blood and guts, you may find *Exterminator 10* entertaining. If not, save your money.

Circle the best answer for each question.

1. Did the reviewer like the movie? Why or why not?
   (1) Yes, because the lead character was so good.
   (2) No, because the special effects were disappointing.
   (3) Yes, because it was an interesting story.
   (4) No, because it was too bloody.

2. Which of the following statements is a fact?

    (1) The *Exterminator* series is too violent.

    (2) At least 24 people die in the first hour of the movie.

    (3) Mack Starr is a cardboard character.

    (4) The special effects are great.

3. Which of the following statements is an opinion?

    (1) Most of the supporting actors are not very good.

    (2) The movie is about drug dealers in South America.

    (3) This is the tenth movie in the series.

    (4) *Exterminator 11* is scheduled to come out next summer.

4. Which of the following statements is a fact?

    (1) Joe Bara does a nice job as the bad guy.

    (2) The plot has few surprises.

    (3) Even the blood looks real.

    (4) There is a scene where the lab blows up.

5. Which of the following statements is an opinion?

    (1) At least two dozen people die in clever, disgusting ways.

    (2) Mack Starr is a third-rate James Bond.

    (3) Save your money.

    (4) all of the above.

Check your answers on pages 142-143.

WRITING WORKSHOP

Brainstorm: Find a Topic

What movies have you seen recently that you reacted strongly to? Choose one to write a movie review about.

Focus: List Your Facts and Opinions

Make a list of facts and opinions about the movie.

Expand: Write a Movie Review

Develop your topic into a review that helps the viewer decide whether to see the movie or not. Remember, the more facts you can use to support your opinions, the stronger your review will be.

CHAPTER 6 | DETECTING BIAS

A commentary writer often wants to influence readers' opinions by slanting the facts and appealing to readers' emotions. The writer might claim, "You take your life in your hands every time you leave your house. You must stop protecting criminals and start protecting victims." The biased writer discusses only one side of an issue. The **bias** can be positive or negative.

A positive bias often comes across in ads and commercials because advertisers have a goal. The writers want to persuade you to buy their product. Ads often appeal to consumers' emotions and self-esteem:

"Buy *Red Silk* perfume, and men will think you're beautiful."

"People who drive *Leopard* sports cars are exciting and adventurous."

These ads don't tell you the negative side of either product. They don't tell you that *Red Silk* perfume could give your skin a rash. And they don't say that a *Leopard* sports car costs about three years' wages and is in the repair shop every month. They want you to see only the good side of the product so that you will buy it.

Political commentaries and editorials can also be biased. Editorial writers choose the facts that will lead readers to share their opinions on issues. When you recognize a writer's bias, you are better equipped to decide whether you agree with what you're reading.

■ Notice the bias in the following campaign speech. Is the bias positive or negative? Underline words and phrases that show you if the candidate's speech shows a positive or negative bias.

Senator Thick's Campaign Speech

My fellow Americans, I am here today to tell you why you must reelect me to a fourth term as senator. I'm sure you know that the worst problem facing our state today is lack of jobs. Many companies have closed their doors, and we need to find a way to open them again. We need to put our people back to work. We must bring more industry to this region.

My opponent's ideas are so wrongheaded. He plans to give huge tax breaks to foreigners who open new companies in our state. How blind and stupid can he be? Doesn't he know that our state should include only companies with American products, American employees, and American owners? Does he want our state to go into more debt to reward outsiders who do not belong here? Isn't he smart enough to know that what's good for our state is newly created American businesses? If you're prepared to throw away our economy to foreigners, elect my opponent. But if you want America to grow stronger, march forward into the future with me, Senator Alvin Q. Thick.

. . . .

Did you underline **wrongheaded, blind, stupid, outsiders who do not belong here, isn't he smart enough, if you're prepared to throw away our economy to foreigners**?

Note that the campaign speech did not present plans or proposals for how to bring new business into the state. Thick's purpose was to make his opponent look bad so that you as a voter would reelect Thick. This is a technique used by many political candidates.

STRATEGY: HOW TO RECOGNIZE BIAS

▶ Determine how many points of view are given. If the writer presents only one side, the writing is biased.

▶ Weigh the facts given. Are they true as far as you know? Or are they really disguised opinions?

▶ Look for loaded words that attempt to get you to respond with your emotions instead of your mind.

▶ Find out who the writer is. What are the writer's qualifications?

Exercise 1

Read the two ads and complete the exercises that follow.

When you're watching TV, do you ignore most of the commercials? Or do ads for soft drinks or fast-food restaurants make you thirsty or hungry? Do they make you think, "Yeah, I'd like to eat a big, fat, chewy chocolate chip cookie right now"?

PART A: BUY THE SMOOTH AIR SHOE!

"Do you want to look, feel, and play basketball like a pro? It's easy. Just buy a pair of Smooth Airs. And you'll be in good company. Most of the teams in the NBA have chosen Smooth Airs. They give you the extra jumping power you need for those slam-dunk shots. I scored 38 points in my last game thanks to Smooth Airs. And they're so comfortable, I even wear them off the court. Smooth Airs—for the good times in your life."

Answer the questions in the space provided.

1. Find three phrases from the ad that show the athlete's bias toward Smooth Airs.

   a. _____

   b. _____

   c. _____

2. Who will you feel like if you buy Smooth Airs?

   _____

PART B: BUY THE SMOOTH AIR SHOE!

"I wouldn't be where I am today if I didn't wear Smooth Air shoes. My feet take a lot of pounding as I walk to work from the train each day. I protect them with Smooth Airs. My feet are not tired when I represent my clients in court. And my feet feel comfortable because of the extra layer of padding built into Smooth Air shoes. If you want your feet to feel like they're walking on air, try Smooth Airs."

Answer the questions below.

1. Find three phrases from the ad that show the woman's bias toward Smooth Air shoes.

a. _____

b. _____

c. _____

2. What does the ad suggest Smooth Airs will do for you? **You may check (✓) more than one.**

_____ **(1)** protect your feet on city pavement

_____ **(2)** make you a better athlete

_____ **(3)** help you meet men

_____ **(4)** help you start a new fashion trend

_____ **(5)** help you feel like a professional woman

Check your answers on page 143.

Exercise 2

Read the commentary and complete the exercise that follows.

How do you feel about heart and liver transplants? If you died, would you want to donate your organs to let someone else live? What do you think about doctors killing animals for medical experiments?

The Man with the Baboon Liver

Recently, doctors in Pittsburgh, Pennsylvania, **transplanted**[1] the liver of a baboon into the body of a dying man who had **hepatitis**.[2] This surgery offers new hope to thousands of people who are suffering from liver disease.

Yet some people think the surgery was a mistake. Animal-rights activists protested the transplant because the baboon had to be killed so that its healthy liver could be used. "Did the baboon consent?" read one sign. The protesters said it was wrong for humans to use other species for body parts. But this is a question of the greater good. The man who received the baboon liver would almost certainly have died sooner.

There is a shortage of suitable human livers for transplant. Also, with a human liver, the hepatitis might come back. The man would have gone through the pain of the operation for nothing. Baboons do not get hepatitis. So using a baboon liver greatly increased the patient's chances of survival.

The doctor who performed the surgery said, "We all love animals. But our passion and our commitment is to human beings." Perhaps the protesters should think about that. Would they feel the same if the patient were their brother? This baboon was raised in a medical lab. Donating its liver was the whole purpose of its life.

Our society has become mature and caring enough so that some states have passed laws that ban killing animals for sport alone. Surely all these animal lives saved more than balance out the loss of one animal.

—Marcus Kendall

---

[1]**transplanted:** transferred an organ from one individual to another
[2]**hepatitis:** inflammation of the liver

Circle *T* for true or *F* for false.

T F **1.** The writer thinks a human life is more valuable than an animal one.

T F **2.** A liver transplant from a human donor would have worked just as well.

T F **3.** The protesters don't think animals should be used for spare parts.

T F **4.** The writer thinks society has gotten crueler to animals in recent years.

T F **5.** The doctor who transplanted the liver hates animals.

Check your answers on page 143.

WRITING WORKSHOP

Brainstorm: Find a Topic

Make a list of products you use. Choose one item to advertise.

Focus: Find Your Bias

What do you like best about the product you chose to advertise? Write a short sentence describing your bias. For example:

▶ Crunch-O peanut butter is the best because it has real, whole peanuts.

▶ Rocco's Gym has so much equipment you never have to wait long to use it.

Expand: Write an Ad

Turn your bias sentence into a short, catchy slogan. Add a few sentences describing the benefits of your product in more detail. Does it make you want to run out and buy the item?

CHAPTER 7 | MAKING INFERENCES

Making an **inference** means using information that is stated directly to figure out a message that is *not* stated directly. It's reading between the lines to see what someone is saying. For example, suppose your brother is moving to a new house and you ask if he wants you to come over and help him pack. He sighs and says, "I have so much to do. I haven't even started packing my stereo equipment yet. Just picking up the rental truck will take a couple of hours. And I have to be out of this apartment by tomorrow afternoon. But I'll manage. I know how busy you are."

Your brother's stated message is that he can manage on his own. But what would you infer from the way he says it and from his tone of voice? His unstated message is that he *does* need help. He probably hopes you'll say, "I'm not that busy. I'll be right over to help you."

Making inferences is something you do every day, almost automatically. How do you know what the unstated message is? It's a kind of detective work. First, you gather clues. Then, you analyze them to see what they mean. Finally, you test your inference against the facts given to see if it makes sense. The next paragraph shows another example of making inferences in everyday life.

Alice had been planning this picnic for days. She spent the morning frying chicken, making potato salad, and squeezing lemons for fresh lemonade. It was important to serve cool foods on a day like this. She picked up Enríque, and they drove to the beach with the air-conditioning on full blast. When they got there, they spread out a tablecloth right next to the water. "I want to work up an appetite," said Alice. She took off her sunglasses and jumped into the lake.

■ What is the weather like for Alice's picnic? What clues (stated details) in the paragraph tell you what you need to know to make the right inference?

_____

_____

Could you tell that it was hot and sunny? The facts—that she served cool foods, turned on the air-conditioning in the car, wore sunglasses, and went for a swim—add up to that conclusion.

Often, the humor in cartoons comes from unstated messages. To get the joke, the reader must use the pictures and words to infer something.

■ Look at the cartoon. What are two facts (not inferences) you observe?

_____

_____

The two people are watching TV. The announcer says, "The following may not be suitable for younger viewers . . . Parental guidance is suggested." The woman seems puzzled. And the man says, "Campaign commercial."

■ Based on these facts, what does the cartoon suggest, or imply?

_____

The cartoon suggests that exposing young children to political ads might have a negative effect on them.

STRATEGY: HOW TO MAKE INFERENCES

▶ Gather clues from the stated message.
▶ Analyze the clues to figure out what they mean.
▶ Test your conclusion against the facts given.
▶ Put all the facts and details together to make an inference.

Exercise 1

Study the cartoon and complete the exercises that follow.

This cartoonist has doubts about the way our government is run. Do you feel the government does enough for its citizens? Are you better or worse off than you were ten years ago?

Choose the correct answers for questions 1–4.

1. Which statements are facts that may be arrived at by the clues shown in the cartoon? **You may check (✓) more than one.**
   - **____ (1)** The newspaper says the rich got richer in the 1980s.
   - **____ (2)** The woman with the shopping cart got richer in the 1980s.
   - **____ (3)** The man in the coat is not one of the rich.
   - **____ (4)** The man in the shabby coat is a newspaper reporter.
   - **____ (5)** The woman isn't hopeful that the 1990s will be better.
   - **____ (6)** The situation takes place in a city.
   - **____ (7)** Poverty is a problem only in the city.

2. Which of the following statements can you *infer* from the newspaper headline? **You may check (✔) more than one.**

____ **(1)** While the rich got richer, the poor got poorer.

____ **(2)** The newspaper is wrong.

____ **(3)** The economic situation is even worse in the 1990s.

____ **(4)** The gap between the rich and the poor has grown.

3. Which of the following statements can you *infer* from looking at the two people in the cartoon? **You may check (✔) more than one.**

____ **(1)** It is summer.

____ **(2)** It is winter.

____ **(3)** The characters live in a rural area.

____ **(4)** The characters live in an urban area.

____ **(5)** These two people are homeless.

____ **(6)** The shopping cart is full of groceries.

____ **(7)** The shopping cart is full of this woman's possessions.

4. The information in the headline is probably based on **(choose only one)**

(1) a politician's campaign speech

(2) a poll taken of voters' beliefs

(3) facts from a government report on income

(4) the opinions of the poor

Answer the question in the space provided.

5. This cartoon's humor depends on the punch line delivered by the woman. What would be the expected response to the man's question, "So, what did the rest of us get?"

_____

Check your answers on page 143.

Exercise 2

Study the cartoon and complete the exercise that follows.

This cartoon talks about the difference in pay for men and women doing the same work. How do you feel about this?

ARLO & JANIS® by Jimmy Johnson

Circle S for a stated fact or I for an inference.

S   I   **1.** Janis admires the salad Arlo made.

S   I   **2.** Janis doesn't really believe that all men are great cooks even though she says she agrees with Arlo.

S   I   **3.** Arlo is proud of his salad-making ability.

S   I   **4.** The child wants to know the difference between a cook and a chef.

S   I   **5.** The point of the cartoon is that women should get equal pay for equal work.

S   I   **6.** Arlo believes that all the great chefs are men.

S   I   **7.** Arlo has a lot of self-confidence.

S   I   **8.** The child has been listening to the adults' conversation.

Check your answers on page 143.

WRITING WORKSHOP

Brainstorm: Gather Clues

In this chapter, you read three cartoons. The first was about a campaign commercial that might be considered objectionable. The second showed a homeless couple in the 1990s reading about how the rich got richer in the 1980s. The third cartoon was about the difference in pay between a male chef and a female cook. You gathered clues in each cartoon to figure out what really was going on.

Do you have a point you'd like to get across through words and images? Make a list of subjects you feel strongly about.

Focus: Choose a Subject

From the list you made, choose one situation to draw a cartoon about. Don't worry about being an artist. You can use stick figures if you like. The important thing is what the cartoon says. You might create a cartoon about

▶ a humorous family incident or vacation

▶ an embarrassing situation

▶ an event that didn't turn out the way you had planned

▶ a funny comment a child made to you

▶ a sports scene

▶ a dinner date that turned into a disaster

▶ a teacher who learned an important lesson

Expand: Write a Paragraph

Develop your situation into a cartoon. Put in enough stated facts so your readers will have something to work with. But don't tell them everything about what your characters think and feel and why they act as they do. Ask several people to read your cartoon. Did they all infer the conclusions you intended? Ask your readers what facts they used to make their inferences.

Unit 2
REVIEW

Read the article and complete the exercise that follows.

Have you ever felt a lot of stress at work, at home, or in school? How did you handle it when you were under pressure?

Secretarial Work Can Cause Stress

Did you know that working women as a group have no higher rate of heart disease than homemakers? But women employed in secretarial jobs do. Their heart disease rate is twice that of other women, says a medical study. This is a real problem, since almost twenty million women have secretarial jobs. Doctors found that the women at greatest risk either had trouble letting their anger show or had bosses who were not supportive. Many of these women also had several children, as well as husbands who worked in blue-collar jobs.

Why are secretaries more likely to have heart problems? Secretaries are under more stress than even busy women managers. And secretaries have a lot of responsibility. They don't get to make very many of their own decisions. They usually have heavy work loads and tight deadlines. Yet secretaries don't get much appreciation for their work. And after a busy day at the office, they are expected to go home and cook, clean, and take care of everyone else's needs. One doctor says, "The evidence is clear. Having to please too many people, and not having control over your life is bad for your health."

The situation is getting worse instead of better. Most secretaries today use computers on the job. Computers have made businesses at least 15 percent more **productive**[1] than they were ten years ago. But while productivity has gone up, secretarial pay has not. Many secretaries do work on a computer that is simple and boring. So, bosses see these jobs as lower-paying positions.

Computers have made clerical workers more isolated from their co-workers, too. This takes away one main stress reliever—complaining about the job. Fears about the health risks of working at a computer screen all day add to stress.

---

[1]productive: yielding results, benefits, or profits

Computers can count keystrokes and measure how much work is done. So this adds to workers' stress level.

Increased stress equals greater risk of heart disease. Some of the solutions are simple. Secretaries can make an effort to get exercise, eat right, and learn to relax. But other solutions are harder to reach. More businesses must learn how to value secretaries and the work they do. But most have not figured out how to do that yet.

· ·

Circle the best answer for each question.

1. Which women have the greatest risk of getting a heart attack?

    (1) those who are managers

    (2) those who can't express anger or who have nonsupportive bosses

    (3) those who use computers

    (4) those who get exercise and eat right

2. Which of the following statements is a fact?

    (1) Everyone thinks computers are wonderful.

    (2) Most businesses have learned to value secretaries.

    (3) Families provide more stress than relaxation.

    (4) Working women as a group have no higher rate of heart disease than homemakers, but secretaries do.

3. Which of the following statements is an opinion?

    (1) Secretaries have twice as much risk of heart attacks as other women do.

    (2) Computers have increased productivity by 15 percent.

    (3) Secretaries like having lots of responsibility.

    (4) Computers can count keystrokes and measure how much work is done.

4. The writer's bias is

    (1) pro secretaries

    (2) anti men

    (3) anti work

    (4) pro bosses

Check your answers on page 143.

UNIT 3
READING POETRY

It might not seem at first glance that poetry is very important. After all, it doesn't usually tell you how to do something or what's happening in the news or what tasks your job calls for. But what poetry does better than any other kind of writing is capture a feeling in words that make the reader feel it, too. A good poem can surprise and delight you or make you laugh or cry.

You may not read poetry very often, but it touches your life anyway. If you listen to any songs that have words, from blues to pop, from rap to rock, you're listening to poetry. As you read the poems in this unit, try to hear them the way you hear a song.

POETRY

TOPICS

Form

- Fog
- Concrete Cat
- Well, Yes
- A Seeing Poem

Rhyme and Rhythm

- The Veteran
- Love
- Two Limericks

Imagery

- Beauty
- Dust of Snow
- Swift Things Are Beautiful

Simile and Metaphor

- Some People
- Night Plane
- Mother to Son
- Joe

AFTER READING THIS UNIT, YOU SHOULD BE ABLE TO
▶ IDENTIFY THE FORM OF A POEM
▶ IDENTIFY RHYME AND RHYTHM
▶ IDENTIFY IMAGERY
▶ RECOGNIZE SIMILE AND METAPHOR

CHAPTER 8 | FORM

When you read a poem, one of the first things you notice is its **form**. That's the way it looks on the page. Form includes the number of lines in each **stanza**, or verse, and how long the lines are. For example, this poem by Carl Sandburg is written in two stanzas:

Fog

The fog comes
on little cat feet.

It sits looking
over harbor and city
on silent haunches
and then moves on.

The length of lines and where they break may have nothing to do with where the sentences end. Instead, they are clues to help you understand the feelings and meanings the poet wants to get across. Where a poet leaves extra space between words or lines, you should pause as you read. Notice the space between the two verses of the poem "Fog."

Many poems are in **free form**, which means they don't follow a set pattern. Sometimes poets play with the placement of words. They make the shape of the poem look like the object the poem is about. These are called **concrete** poems. The following poem by Dorothi Charles is a good example:

Concrete Cat

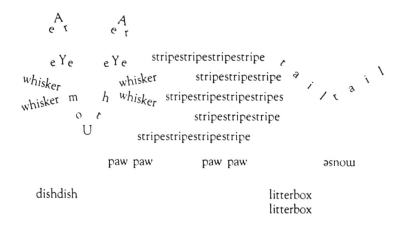

Did the meaning of this poem hit you before you even thought about it? Did you see the shape of the cat as you read the words? If so, the poem has succeeded.

■ Answer the questions in the space provided.

Why did the poet capitalize the *As* in the ears and the *U* in the mouth?

_____

It was to show the pointed shape of the ears and the rounded shape of the mouth.

What words in the poem are not parts of a cat?

_____

The words are **dish**, **litterbox**, and **mouse**.

What sense does this poem appeal to?

_____

It appeals to the sense of sight.

STRATEGY: UNDERSTANDING FORM

▶ Notice the way the poem looks on the page before you even begin to read it.
▶ Is the poem broken into stanzas, or verses? If so, each verse will be about a part of an idea.
▶ Do the words in the poem form the shape of an object?
▶ After you read through the poem, think about the feeling it gives you. Does its form add to that feeling?

Exercise 1

Read the poem and complete the exercise that follows.

Do you like candy bars? Does this poem make you hungry for one?

Well, Yes
Candy bar—

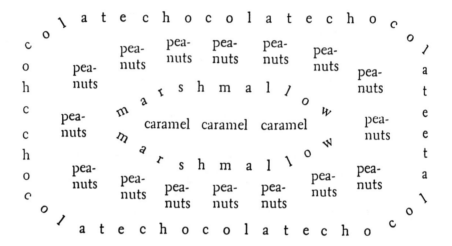

Too much.
Too much.
But I'll have one more.

—by Robert Froman

Circle the best answer for each question.

1. In what way does the arrangement of the words in the poem look like a candy bar?
   (1) The word *chocolate* is printed over and over again in the rectangular shape of a candy bar.
   (2) The words are layered like the parts of a candy bar.
   (3) The chocolate is on the outside, and the other ingredients are on the inside.
   (4) all of the above

2. What senses does this poem appeal to?
   (1) smell and hearing
   (2) sight and smell
   (3) sight and taste
   (4) touch and taste

3. What do the last three lines of the poem mean?
   (1) The speaker had too many candy bars.
   (2) The speaker feels full but will have another candy bar.
   (3) The speaker will not eat any more candy bars.
   (4) The speaker doesn't like to eat candy bars.

4. The candy bar in the poem contains what four ingredients?
   (1) peanut butter, marshmallow, chocolate, raisins
   (2) peanuts, chocolate, coconut, marshmallow
   (3) chocolate, almonds, marshmallow, peanuts
   (4) chocolate, peanuts, caramel, marshmallow

5. Which candy bar contains *most* of the ingredients shown in the poem?
   (1) Hershey Bar
   (2) Butterfinger
   (3) Snickers
   (4) PayDay

Check your answers on page 143.

Exercise 2

Read the poem and complete the exercise that follows.

What does the shape of this poem remind you of? Does it turn on a light in your mind?

A Seeing Poem

—by Robert Froman

Circle the best answer for each question.

1. Why did the poet capitalize the letters of the words in his poem?
   (1) to show that all the letters in the poem have the same importance
   (2) to show that all the words in the poem have the same importance
   (3) because he likes capital letters better than small ones
   (4) because he wanted the words to flow

2. What sense does this poem appeal to most?
   (1) smell
   (2) hearing
   (3) sight
   (4) taste

3. What do you think was the author's main purpose in writing this poem?
   (1) to persuade readers to buy light bulbs
   (2) to inspire readers to create their own poems
   (3) to describe why each poem should have a concrete shape
   (4) to entertain readers and surprise them

Check your answers on page 143.

WRITING WORKSHOP

Brainstorm: Find a Topic

Three of the four poems you read in this chapter were concrete poems. The words in the concrete poems were put together to form the shape of the object they were describing. Make a list of objects you would like to write a poem about.

Focus: Write Down Details

Choose one object for your poem. Make a list of words or phrases that describe the object. For example, cloud: *fluffy, white, high, soft, airy, constantly moving.*

Expand: Write a Concrete Poem

Now that you have chosen an object and the details you want to include, write a poem. Then write the words so they form the shape of the object you're describing. You will have written a concrete poem.

CHAPTER 9 | RHYME AND RHYTHM

The first things you notice about many poems are rhyme and rhythm. **Rhythm** is all around us. Your heart beats in a steady rhythm. The pace at which you walk has its own rhythm. If you're in the habit of tapping a pencil when you're thinking, you tap in a rhythm.

If you stop wherever you are and listen, you'll probably hear something rhythmic. It might be the song of a bird or the tick of a clock or the clackety-clack of a subway train. And, of course, the beat of whatever music you listen to is its rhythm.

Poets create rhythm in different ways. It may come from the number of syllables in a line or from repeating certain words. It may come from echoing certain sounds. For example, in "*Peter Piper picked a peck of pickled peppers*," the rhythm comes from the fact that most of the words start with *p*. Another way poets create rhythm is by using words that rhyme, either at the end of lines or within lines.

When we say two words **rhyme**, it means they sound alike at the end of each word. For example, "the *moon* in *June*" is a rhyme. So is "the *cat* in the *hat*." Different kinds of poems have different rhyme patterns. Here's an example:

> I eat my peas with honey.
> I've done it all my life.
> They do taste kind of funny,
> But it keeps them on the knife.

That poem has a very common rhyme scheme. The first line rhymes with the third, and the second line rhymes with the fourth. Another popular rhyme scheme is the limerick. In it, the first, second, and fifth lines rhyme with each other, and the third and fourth lines rhyme. The writers of most limericks are **anonymous**, or unknown.

Before people could write things down, both rhyme and rhythm helped them remember stories. They can help you remember poems you like today. Once you know a poem by heart, it belongs to you forever.

In a good poem, rhyme and rhythm don't take up so much of your attention that you miss what the poem is about. Instead, they add to its meaning. Look at the two limericks that follow.

There was a young lady of **Lynn**[1]
Who was so uncommonly thin
That when she **essayed**[2]
To drink lemonade
She slipped through the straw and fell in.

A boy who weighed many an **oz.**[3]
Used language I will not pronoz.
His sister one day
Pulled his chair right away
She wanted to see if he'd boz.

■ Based on the two limericks, answer the questions below.

Which words rhyme with each other in the first limerick?

_____

the second limerick? _____

In the first limerick, *Lynn*, *thin*, and *in* rhyme and *essayed* and *lemonade* rhyme.

The second limerick is a bit trickier. In the first line, the word *ounce* is abbreviated to *oz.* You've probably seen that before. But the unusual thing is that the words that rhyme with ounce—*pronounce* and *bounce*, are also abbreviated. **So, in this limerick, *oz.*, *pronoz.*, and *boz.* rhyme. *Day* and *away* also rhyme.**

Both limericks have the same rhyme pattern. They also have the same rhythm. You may have noticed that lines 1 and 2 are long (eight syllables each). Lines 3 and 4 are short (five syllables each).

How long is line 5 in the poems? _____

Line 5 has eight syllables. It's the same length as lines 1 and 2. It has the same rhythm as those lines.

STRATEGY: HOW TO IDENTIFY RHYTHM AND RHYME

▶ As you read the poem out loud, listen for the beat. Can you hear a rhythm?

▶ Look for words that are repeated.

▶ Look for series of words that start with the same letter.

▶ Does the last word in each line sound like the end of another line?

▶ Look for rhyming words within lines, too.

---

[1]**Lynn:** a city in Massachusetts
[2]**essayed:** tried
[3]**oz.:** ounce ($\frac{1}{16}$ of a pound)

Exercise 1

Read the poem and complete the exercise that follows.

Have your attitudes toward right and wrong changed over the years?
How about your beliefs about what's worth fighting for?

The Veteran

When I was young and bold and strong,
Oh, right was right, and wrong was wrong!
My **plume**[1] on high, my flag **unfurled**,[2]
I rode away to right the world.
5   "Come out, you dogs, and fight!" said I,
And wept there was but once to die.

But I am old; and good and bad
Are woven in a crazy plaid.
I sit and say, "The world is so;
10   And he is wise who lets it go.
A battle lost, a battle won—
The difference is small, my son."

—by Dorothy Parker

---

[1]plume: a feather-shaped token of honor
[2]unfurled: unfolded and flying in the breeze

Circle _T_ if the statement is true or _F_ if it is false.

T F **1.** In the first verse, the words that rhyme include _high_ and _right_.

T F **2.** When the speaker was young, she wanted to save the world.

T F **3.** Now that the speaker is old, she fights even harder to do the right thing.

T F **4.** The pattern here is that lines 1 and 2 rhyme, as do lines 3 and 4, and lines 5 and 6.

T F **5.** The speaker can no longer tell right from wrong.

T F **6.** The speaker was never willing to die for her beliefs.

T F **7.** The rhythm and number of syllables are about the same in every line.

T F **8.** Among the rhyming words are _bad_ and _plaid_.

Circle the best answer for the question.

9. Which sentence best sums up the main idea of this poem?
   (1) When she was young, the speaker just didn't care about what was right or wrong.
   (2) In old age, the speaker cares deeply about convincing people of her point of view.
   (3) Now that she is old, the speaker sees that every issue has some good and some bad in it.
   (4) In old age, the speaker has taken up weaving plaid fabrics.

Check your answers on page 144.

Exercise 2

Read the poem and complete the exercise that follows.

This poem lists many different kinds of love. Which kinds can you identify with?

Love

There's the wonderful love of a beautiful maid,
    And the love of a **staunch**[1] true man,
And the love of a baby that's unafraid—
    All have existed since time began.

5   But the most wonderful love, the Love of all loves,
       Even greater than the love for Mother,
    Is the **infinite**,[2] tenderest, **passionate**[3] love
       Of one dead drunk for another.

—Anonymous

Circle the best answer for each question.

1. What is the rhyme pattern of this poem?
   (1) Lines 1 and 3 rhyme, and lines 2 and 4 rhyme.
   (2) Lines 1 and 2 rhyme, and lines 3 and 4 rhyme.
   (3) The first and last lines rhyme.
   (4) It's not a rhyming poem.

2. The feeling this poet is trying for is
   (1) funny
   (2) sad
   (3) suspicious
   (4) none of the above

---

[1]staunch: loyal
[2]infinite: endless
[3]passionate: strong and intense

3. The poem claims the greatest love of all is

    (1) a beautiful girl's love

    (2) a loyal man's love

    (3) a mother's love

    (4) a drunk's love

4. The last line of the poem

    (1) is designed to make readers cry

    (2) is a punch line

    (3) rhymes with the first line

    (4) has a different rhythm from the rest

5. Part of the poem's rhythm comes from the way it keeps repeating what word?

    (1) wonderful

    (2) Mother

    (3) all

    (4) love

Check your answers on page 144.

WRITING WORKSHOP

Brainstorm: Choose a Topic

Think of some subjects that interest you enough to write about. For example, are you a baseball fan? Do you like to cook? Do you like to visit the zoo? Choose one interest to write about.

Focus: Make a List of Rhymes

Now that you have a topic, think about words that rhyme with it. For example, suppose you like to visit the zoo. Imagine you are an animal in a cage. How would you feel? Make a list of words that rhyme with *zoo*: *new, do, true*. Then make rhyming lists for several other key words you want to use in your poem.

Expand: Write a Poem

Now plug in your rhyming words at the end of lines where you need them. For example, "I wonder what I'll *do*/said the tiger in the *zoo*./They're moving me to a new *cage*/so I might fly into a *rage*./ I'll attack everyone in *sight*/And cause a terrible *fright*."

Your poem does not have to rhyme as this one does. Look back through the poems you've already read and notice their different rhyme patterns.

CHAPTER 10 | **IMAGERY**

Poets use words the way artists use paints, to create pictures in the minds of their readers. Using words to describe something so clearly that you can see it is called **imagery**.

But sight is not the only sense that poets use. They also may describe their world in terms that make you hear, taste, smell, and touch it. They try to appeal to all your senses.

Imagine yourself walking down a city street in the summertime. Can you feel the muggy air on your skin? Can you taste the grit in the air from too much traffic? Can you smell hot dogs or other foods people are eating outside at lunchtime?

Think about what words you would use to describe your city to somebody who has never been there. Poets choose these words and then put them together in ways so vivid that the scenes they're describing come to life for their readers. Then they may use those scenes to make a point about their experiences or beliefs. Poems have many different ways of helping us see more clearly.

The poem below also captures an image and uses it to make a point. Its second verse, or stanza, shows how the poet felt when he saw the image.

Dust of Snow

The way a crow
Shook down on me
The dust of snow
From a **hemlock**[1] tree

5   Has given my heart
A change of mood
And saved some part
Of a day I had **rued**.[2]

—by Robert Frost

---

[1]**hemlock:** an evergreen tree
[2]**rued:** regretted

■ What image does Frost want you to see in your mind's eye?

_____

_____

If you said **a crow landing in an evergreen tree with enough force to shake loose some of the snow on the branches**, you have a good idea of what Frost meant.

■ Can you put yourself in the poet's place and imagine what your other senses would experience in this scene?

_____

Did you imagine **feeling cold, wet snow against your skin? Breathing crisp, dry air? Seeing the blackness of the crow contrasted against the whiteness of the snow**?

■ In the second verse, the poet uses that same image to make a larger point. When he says it has given his heart a change of mood, do you think it made him happier or sadder?

_____

It made him happier. Frost is suggesting that some small event can cheer you up no matter how big your problems seem. In fact, seeing this one example of nature's beauty turned his whole day around.

STRATEGY: IDENTIFYING IMAGERY

▶ As you read the poem, look for words that appeal to your senses.
▶ Try to put yourself inside the world of the poem. See, hear, touch, taste, and smell the things it describes.
▶ When you see an interesting image in life, think of words you would choose to share it with a friend.

Exercise 1

Read the poem and complete the exercise that follows.

When you look around you, where do you find beauty? Can you see it in the everyday things as this Native American woman does?

Beauty

Beauty is seen
In the sunlight,
The trees, the birds,
Corn growing and people working
5   Or dancing for their harvest.

Beauty is heard
In the night,
Wind sighing, rain falling,
Or a singer chanting
10   Anything in **earnest**.[1]

Beauty is in yourself.
Good deeds, happy thoughts
That repeat themselves
In your dreams,
15   In your work,
And even in your rest.

—by E-Yeh-Shure

---

[1]earnest: a serious state of mind

Answer the questions in the space provided.

1. What sense does the poet appeal to in the first verse?

_____

2. What sense does she appeal to in the second verse?

_____

3. In the third verse, where else does the poet say a person can find beauty?

_____

_____

4. What images does the poet use in the first verse to describe beauty?

_____

_____

5. What time of day does the second verse describe?

_____

6. How many verses does this poem have?

_____

7. In what way is the third verse different from verses 1 and 2?

_____

8. What do you notice about the last word in each verse?

_____

Check your answers on page 144.

Exercise 2

Read the poem and complete the exercise that follows.

This is another poet's list of things she finds beautiful. As you read, see if you and the poet have any similar images about things that are beautiful.

Swift Things Are Beautiful

Swift things are beautiful:
Swallows and deer,
And lightning that falls
Bright-veined and clear,
5 River and meteors,
Wind in the wheat,
The strong-**withered**¹ horse,
The runner's sure feet.

And slow things are beautiful:
10 The closing of day,
The pause of the wave
That curves downward to spray,
The **ember**² that crumbles,
The opening flower
15 And the ox that moves on
In the quiet of power.

—by Elizabeth Coatsworth

Answer the questions in the space provided.

1. What images does the poet use in the first verse to show that swift things can be beautiful?

_____

_____

---

¹withers: the ridge between the shoulder bones of a horse
²ember: glowing coal

2. What images does the poet use in the second verse to show that slow things can be beautiful?

_____

_____

3. What sense does the poet appeal to in both verses?

_____

4. Choose one image from the first verse and tell why you think the poet might describe it as beautiful.

_____

_____

5. Choose one image from the second verse and tell why you think the poet might describe it as beautiful.

_____

_____

Check your answers on page 144.

WRITING WORKSHOP

Brainstorm: Make a List of Things You Find Beautiful

Think about something in your own life that you find beautiful. Make notes about the images that come to your mind.

Expand: Write a Poem

Use these images in a poem about things you consider beautiful. You might choose to concentrate on one thing, or you might want to list several things.

Focus: Study Your Images

Go back over your poem and see if you appealed to your readers' senses. Make your images as clear and vivid as you can. Now ask a friend to read your poem. Can he or she walk into the world you've described?

CHAPTER 11 | SIMILE AND METAPHOR

Poets often compare two things. When they describe something their readers are not familiar with, they might compare it to something readers do know.

A **simile** spells out this comparison by using words such as *like*, *as*, and *as if*. For example, suppose you say of an athlete, "He moves like the wind." People know you don't mean that he's invisible or he knocks leaves off trees. You mean just that he's very fast.

A **metaphor** also compares two unlike things, but it doesn't use *like* or *as*. For example, suppose you read, "The moon is a silver platter." You know perfectly well that the moon is *not* a silver platter. It's a sphere of rocks and dirt several million miles away. But this metaphor lets you imagine what the moon looks like to the poet. It also lets you know that the moon in this description is full, not a crescent moon or a half-moon.

Poets use simile and metaphor for many of the same reasons that they use imagery. Such language can be the most effective way to get across a feeling and a deeper meaning. Simile and metaphor can take an unclear idea and turn it into an image you can see and touch and, therefore, understand.

Notice the simile that extends through both verses of the following poem.

Night Plane

. . . .

> The midnight plane with its riding lights
> looks like a **footloose**[1] star
> wandering west through the blue-black night
> to where the mountains are,
>
> 5   a star that's journeyed nearer earth
> to tell each quiet farm
> and little town, "Put out your lights,
> children of earth. Sleep warm."

—by Frances M. Frost

. . . .

---

[1]**footloose:** free to move around

■ Based on the poem "Night Plane," answer the questions below.

What does the poet compare the midnight plane to?

_____

If you said *a footloose star* (**line 2**), you're right.

Is line 2 a simile or a metaphor? _____

It's a simile, because it uses the word *like*.

Simile and metaphor can also add emotional strength to a statement. If you say about a co-worker, "Joe Shmoe is a weasel" (a metaphor), you are not claiming that Joe is really a furry, four-legged animal. But you are successfully conveying your opinion that Joe can't be trusted. When Paul Simon sang, "She loves me like a rock" (a simile), he was saying her love is solid and dependable.

STRATEGY: HOW TO RECOGNIZE SIMILES AND METAPHORS

▶ Look for the words *like*, *as*, and *as if*.

▶ Look for comparisons between two unlike things.

▶ Picture each image. Notice what is fresh and different about each comparison.

Exercise 1

Read the poem and complete the exercise that follows.

Can you remember some important advice that one of your parents gave you when you were little? Do you have words of wisdom you would like to pass on to your children or to a friend?

Mother to Son

Well, son, I'll tell you:
Life for me ain't been no crystal stair.
It's had tacks in it,
And splinters,

5   And boards torn up,
And places with no carpet on the floor—
Bare.
But all the time
I'se been a-climbin' on,

10   And reachin' landin's,
And turnin' corners,
And sometimes goin' in the dark
Where there ain't been no light.
So, boy, don't you turn back.

15   Don't you set down on the steps
'Cause you find it kinder hard.
Don't you fall now—
For I'se still goin', honey,
I'se still climbin',

20   And life for me ain't been no crystal stair.

—by Langston Hughes

Circle the best answer for each question.

1. What do you think sums up the meaning of this poem?
   (1) The mother wants her son to be a carpenter.
   (2) The mother doesn't want her son to give up in hard times.
   (3) The mother lives in a fifth-floor apartment.
   (4) The mother is worried that her son may be afraid of heights.

2. How do the lengths of the lines relate to the subject of the poem?
   (1) They don't.
   (2) They vary as the mother and son get closer and farther apart.
   (3) They make the reader short of breath as climbing stairs might.
   (4) They resemble steps, longest at the bottom and shortest at the top, with one landing (line 7).

3. What do you think the poet intended readers to see in their mind's eye when they read this poem?
   (1) the mother running up a flight of gleaming glass steps
   (2) the son sitting on the steps relaxing
   (3) the mother trudging up a dark, dingy stairway
   (4) the place at the top of the stairs

Answer the questions in the space provided.

4. Do you think the mother has had an easy life or a hard one? What words make you think so?

   _____

5. Is the mother's advice encouraging or discouraging? What makes you think so?

   _____

   _____

Check your answers on pages 144-145.

Exercise 2

Read the poem and complete the exercise that follows.

Are there people in your life who make you feel good just by being around you? Are there those who tend to make you feel bad?

Some People

Isn't it strange some people make
    You feel so tired inside,
Your thoughts begin to shrivel up
    Like leaves all brown and dried!

5 But when you're with some other ones,
    It's stranger still to find
Your thoughts as thick as fireflies
    All shiny in your mind!

—by Rachel Field

Circle *T* if the statement is true or *F* if it is false.

T F **1.** Both verses compare your thoughts to something else.

T F **2.** The comparison in the first verse is to tiredness.

T F **3.** The comparison in the first verse is a simile.

T F **4.** The comparison in the second verse is a metaphor.

T F **5.** The image described in the second verse is a positive, joyful one.

T F **6.** The image described in the first verse is a cheerful, happy one.

T F **7.** Lines 1 and 3 rhyme.

T F **8.** Lines 1 and 4 rhyme.

T F **9.** Lines 2 and 4 rhyme.

T F **10.** The poet talks about thoughts that are as many and shiny as fireflies.

Check your answers on page 145.

WRITING WORKSHOP

Brainstorm: List Similes and Metaphors

Turn the items below into metaphors or similes by completing the sentences.

The color green is _____.

The bus during rush hour is like _____.

A hot shower is _____.

A deadline at work is like _____.

A hummingbird is _____.

A spider is like _____.

The sound of people fighting is like _____.

The smile on a person's face is _____.

Focus: Choose a Topic

Choose the simile you like best from the list above. What other images and feelings does it bring to mind? Write a paragraph describing the subject you picked. Include details that appeal to all the senses.

Expand: Write a Poem

Now that you have described your scene in a paragraph, turn it into poetry. Add line breaks, white space, rhymes, or anything else that helps to get your message across. Read your poem out loud. Does it flow? Does it paint a picture? How many similes and metaphors have you used?

UNIT 3
REVIEW

Read the poem and complete the exercise that follows.

Do you like to watch birds? Do you feed birds or ducks or chipmunks?
How do you feel about a trip to the zoo?

Joe

We feed the birds in winter,
And outside in the snow
We have a tray of many seeds
For many birds of many breeds
5   And one gray squirrel named Joe.

But Joe comes early,
Joe comes late,
And all the birds
Must stand and wait.
10   And waiting there for Joe to go
Is pretty cold work in the snow.

—by David McCord

Circle the best answer for each question.

1. What is the main idea of this poem?
  (1) The speaker feeds many different kinds of birds.
  (2) The squirrel is greedy and eats the birds' food.
  (3) The birds need food most in the winter.
  (4) The birds don't like the squirrel.

2. Who is Joe?
  (1) the speaker
  (2) the hungriest bird
  (3) the person who feeds the birds
  (4) the squirrel

3. What can you say about this poem's form?

    (1) The number of words changes from line to line.

    (2) The lines gradually get longer from first to last, like stairs.

    (3) Each line is a sentence.

    (4) The poet left extra space after some words to make a point.

4. What is the rhyme scheme of the first verse?

    (1) Lines 1 and 3 rhyme, and lines 2 and 4 rhyme.

    (2) It doesn't rhyme.

    (3) Lines 2 and 5 rhyme, and lines 3 and 4 rhyme.

    (4) The first and last lines rhyme.

5. What is the rhyme pattern of the second verse?

    (1) Lines 6 and 7 rhyme.

    (2) Lines 6 and 8 rhyme.

    (3) Lines 7 and 9 rhyme, and lines 10 and 11 rhyme.

    (4) Lines 6, 8, and 10 rhyme.

6. What picture does the poem paint in your mind?

    (1) birds standing around shivering, waiting to eat

    (2) a tray on top of the snow that has all different shapes and colors of seeds

    (3) a big gray squirrel "elbowing his way" to the food tray

    (4) all of the above

7. What metaphor can you see in the overall meaning of the poem?

    (1) The squirrel is a bully.

    (2) The birds are many different kinds of cars.

    (3) The birdfeeder is the planet Earth.

    (4) The person who feeds the birds is God.

8. In what season does the poem take place? How do you know?

    (1) The poem mentions summer and sand.

    (2) The poem mentions spring and birds.

    (3) The poem mentions winter and snow.

    (4) The poem mentions fall and leaves.

Check your answers on page 145.

UNIT 4
READING
SHORT FICTION

A short story is a form of **fiction**. It is a made-up story from the author's imagination. It describes people, places, and events that the writer invents.

Most stories have at least one character, a setting, a plot, conflict, and a theme or main idea. The people in a story are its **characters**. The **setting** is where and when the story takes place. The **plot** is the series of events that makes up the story. **Conflict** is the problem that the story characters face. The **theme** of a story is its main idea. It is often a message about life or human nature. Figuring out what the author meant from hints and clues is part of the fun of reading fiction.

The main purpose of reading fiction is pleasure. A good story entertains you. It also gives you a look at other kinds of people and how they live. Reading fiction lets you share their experiences and feel what they feel.

SHORT FICTION
TOPICS

Character

- The Eyes of Mr. Lovides

Setting

- An American Twenty

Plot

- The Wallet

Conflict

- 232-9979

Theme and Main Idea

- Two Were Left
- Appalachian Home

AFTER READING THIS UNIT, YOU SHOULD BE ABLE TO

▶ UNDERSTAND HOW CHARACTERS ARE DEVELOPED IN A STORY

▶ UNDERSTAND THE IMPORTANCE OF SETTING IN A STORY

▶ IDENTIFY THE PLOT OF A STORY

▶ IDENTIFY CONFLICT IN A STORY

▶ DETERMINE THE THEME/MAIN IDEA OF A STORY

CHAPTER 12 | CHARACTER

When you really get involved in a work of fiction, it unfolds in your mind like a movie on a screen. You use your own imagination to take the clues the author gives you and turn them into pictures in your mind.

Among the most important things you must be able to picture in a story are its **characters**. The people you meet in stories can be just like people you know. Or they can be people so different from you that you've never run across them in real life. They can even be aliens from the far future. What all good story characters have in common is that you care about them. This makes you care about what happens to them in the story.

Think about how you react when you meet someone for the first time. You notice how the person is dressed, how he or she talks, and other details. You use these clues to help decide whether you like this person. Authors do the same thing in fiction. They give you enough information about their characters so you can decide how you feel about them. Writers do this in two ways. They describe characters' physical appearances and personalities. They also show how characters act and what they say.

The following paragraph is about a fictional character named Herb Stone. Use the details of Herb's appearance and the way he behaves to form a picture of him in your mind.

Hot Herb

Herb looked in the men's-room mirror as he combed his hair. He could still cover his bald spot, but just barely. Maybe it was time to think about a hairpiece. What woman would want a middle-aged, middle-income guy with a bald spot and a beer belly?

"Cut it out, buddy," he said to himself. "This is no time to lose your confidence." He tucked the comb into his pocket, tightened his stomach muscles, and walked out to the bar. "Come on, girls," he yelled above the music. "I'm hot tonight. And I'm buying the drinks."

Pam looked at Herb as he sat down next to her. She thought, "Here comes another loudmouth. Just what I need."

But Herb said, "Hi. I'm Herb Stone. You look like you've had a hard day. Can I buy you a drink?"

Pam said, "Why not? I'd like that. Get me a glass of white wine."

As they talked, Herb and Pam both realized they had a lot in common. They not only lived in the same part of the city, but they also both worked in the downtown area. Herb relaxed and dropped his "Mr. Confidence" act. Pam liked how comfortable she felt with Herb. She discovered they both liked old movies, walks along the lake, Thai food, and garage sales. Pam decided maybe all men weren't jerks after all.

· ·

■ Based on the passage, answer the following questions.

From Herb's description, can you tell how he looks? Which words tell you?

_____

If you said **middle-aged**, **bald spot**, and **beer belly**, you're right.

Now, can you tell from what Herb says and does how he feels about his appearance?

_____

Herb tries to hide his bald spot and suck in his stomach. This shows that Herb is insecure about his looks. Some of what he says confirms it: "This is no time to lose your confidence." Also, "I'm buying the drinks" suggests that he's not sure women will like him for himself.

Based on the passage, what does Pam think about Herb when she first meets him?

_____

You are correct if you said **Pam thinks Herb is just another loudmouthed guy.**

At the end of the passage, how do Pam's thoughts and feelings about Herb change?

_____

You are correct if you said **Pam feels comfortable talking with Herb and realizes she and Herb have a lot in common.**

STRATEGY: UNDERSTANDING CHARACTER

▶ Picture the characters in your mind as you read their physical descriptions.
▶ Notice what the characters do. How does this information add to your picture?
▶ Notice what the characters say and how they say it.
▶ Notice what others in the story say and think about a character.

Exercise

Read the story and complete the activity that follows.

It's said that "the eyes are the windows of the soul." Why are the eyes of Mr. Lovides important to this story?

The Eyes of Mr. Lovides

by John Godey

It was a quarter to ten, and the breakfast was over. But Joey **dawdled**,[1] inventing aimless tasks for himself, dreading the moment when he would have to approach Mr. Lovides, although Frank had assured him there would be no difficulty.

Even after a year in the employ of Mr. Lovides, Joey still feared him. Mr. Lovides had olive skin (much darker than Joey's own) and hollow cheeks with sharply etched lines. He was a **taciturn**[2] man who never smiled.

But it was the eyes of Mr. Lovides that made Joey afraid. They were black eyes, not bright and polished as eyes should be, but like **pitch**,[3] set deep and hot in the bony sockets. Joey did not understand these eyes; they appeared always to be threatening. He had mentioned this once to Frank. Frank had laughed and said that in his opinion the eyes of Mr. Lovides seemed rather gentle and compassionate.

Joey glanced at the clock once more and became panicky. If he did not leave soon he would be late, and the ceremony would be delayed.

He straightened his shoulders, wiped his moist hands on his apron and walked forward on the slat platform to the cashier's desk at the front of the luncheonette. Mr. Lovides sat behind the desk, with a sheaf of statements and his big checkbook before him. He looked up at Joey.

Joey's gaze wavered before Mr. Lovides's flat stare. He wet his lips with his tongue and managed to blurt out, "Frank said he speak to you, ask you to let me off for his marriage. To be witness."

---

¹dawdled: moved slowly
²taciturn: quiet, not talkative
³pitch: black tar

Mr. Lovides's lids flickered for a moment, concealing his eyes. "Be back by eleven-thirty," he said.

Joey turned away quickly and went back to the kitchen. He dressed swiftly but with care, putting on the powder-blue suit with the thin stripes running through the cloth like rich veins of gold.

Mr. Lovides did not look up from the cashier's desk as he hurried by.

Joey waited impatiently on the el platform for a train. When it came, he took a seat beside a window.

The train moved rapidly in its halting, deceptively **antiquated**[4] way, and in another ten minutes it would be there. The realization that he would soon be seeing Frank for the last time filled his eyes with sudden tears. He brushed them away angrily. A wedding day was not a day for tears, but for rejoicing.

Yet for Joey it was a day of sorrow. Without Frank he could not hope to hold the job of counterman. Soon he would be back in the sweaty kitchen again.

In the beginning he had not minded the dishwashing. He had left Puerto Rico only a week before he got the job. Any job was fine which would pay enough to live on, to buy the splendid, sharp clothing worn by his **compatriots**[5] in the States. The trays heaped with soiled dishes were a heavy load. The smells of the kitchen were sometimes overpowering. The hot, greasy dishwater reddened and wrinkled his hands. But it had seemed a fine job—then.

He could not now recall the first time Frank had spoken to him. Joey's English had been very poor then, and he would not have understood Frank anyway. But he did understand the friendly tone of Frank's voice and the warm smile of this tall counterman with the blond, unruly hair. It was the first friendliness he had encountered in the **teeming**,[6] hostile city.

He cherished the countless instances of Frank's warmth and helpfulness, but the most memorable of all came on the day Ralph, the second counterman, quit. Frank went to Mr. Lovides and asked him to try Joey at the job. Mr. Lovides had at first been unwilling to do this, but he had much respect for Frank. The next morning Joey came out of the kitchen and took his place proudly behind the second counter.

Joey was polite and cheerful, and he soon built up his own circle of special customers. Many of them were girls—stenographers and clerks from the big office buildings—who enjoyed making him blush by remarking on his long black eyelashes. Oh, it was a wonderful job. He was no longer a menial, an unskilled boy from Puerto Rico, but a personage of some importance. . . .

4antiquated: old
5compatriots: countrymen
6teeming: crowded

The train had come into the City Hall Station. Joey got out and went slowly down the stairs to the street. Even now, he found it hard to believe that Frank was going away, though he had known for a long time that his friend planned to be married and then return to his home in Worcester to live.

As Frank's last day at the luncheonette came closer, Joey had grown increasingly **morose**.[7] He had even been rude to one of his regular customers. Mr. Lovides had witnessed the incident. He said nothing, but the look in his eyes had burned fear into Joey's heart. The fear was still with him as he entered the building where Frank was waiting. . . .

The marriage didn't take long. A white-haired man intoned the phrases, while Frank and his girl looked at each other with glistening eyes. Frank and his new wife smiled at Joey warmly and insisted that he come up to Worcester often to visit them. He stood there and nodded, his eyes filled with tears, the smile on his lips fixed and stiff. Then they were gone, and he walked back to the el and returned to the luncheonette.

His legs trembled as he opened the door and went in. His eyes picked out the wall clock: 11:25. He started toward the kitchen and then stopped, as abruptly as though he had come up against an invisible barrier. Behind the counter—the second counter, *his* counter—there was another man, wearing a fresh linen jacket.

For a long time Joey stood still, feeling the heat of unreleased tears behind his blinking lids. Nor did he move when Mr. Lovides came out of the kitchen and walked toward him.

He was only dimly aware of Mr. Lovides's voice: "Got a new man to work the second counter . . ."

It had happened already, so soon. The very day of Frank's departure he had become again a Puerto Rican boy of no **consequence**,[8] fit only for the kitchen, the greasy suds. Without Frank, he was nothing.

The eyes of Mr. Lovides drilled into him, but his voice was lost in the roaring that filled Joey's ears. A wave of self-pitying resentment surged up in him. But suddenly Mr. Lovides's voice penetrated Joey's **anguish**.[9] Joey stared at him in disbelief.

Mr. Lovides, somewhat impatiently, repeated himself: "So from now on you work the first counter. Understand?"

---

[7]morose: sad
[8]consequence: importance
[9]anguish: pain

Joey could not trust himself to reply. He nodded his head in **mute**,[10] overwhelming happiness. Now he could bear the going away of Frank, now he could bear anything that might come. He was no longer an **alien**,[11] but a man who could stand alone, in confidence and pride. He had lost much today, when Frank had gone away. But he had gained even more than he had lost.

Before starting for the kitchen, Joey looked directly into the eyes of Mr. Lovides. They were gentle, compassionate eyes, and he was astonished that he could ever have feared them.

....

Circle the best answer for each question.

1. How many characters are named in the story?

(1) one

(2) two

(3) three

(4) four

2. What does Joey think of Mr. Lovides at the beginning of the story?

(1) that he's frightening

(2) that he's kind

(3) that he's frightened

(4) that he's stupid

3. In the last three paragraphs of the story, what does Joey realize about Mr. Lovides's character?

(1) He's cruel.

(2) He's shy.

(3) He's kind.

(4) He's prejudiced.

4. Frank does not share Joey's original opinion of Mr. Lovides. What does Frank say his eyes are like?

(1) mean and threatening

(2) black as pitch

(3) concealed

(4) gentle and compassionate

---

[10]**mute:** silent

[11]**alien:** foreigner

5. What kind of person is Frank?

   (1) warm and friendly

   (2) a bully

   (3) shy and quiet

   (4) prejudiced against Puerto Ricans

6. What kind of clothes does Joey like?

   (1) jeans and T-shirts

   (2) leather jackets

   (3) sharp, dressy clothes

   (4) He's not interested in clothes.

7. The next-to-last paragraph says Joey "had gained even more than he had lost." What does Joey gain at the end of the story?

   (1) money

   (2) confidence and pride

   (3) a wife

   (4) knowledge of how to fight

8. Which trait does *not* describe Joey?

   (1) insecure

   (2) Puerto Rican

   (3) shy

   (4) confident

9. Which trait does *not* describe Frank?

   (1) has long black eyelashes

   (2) is tall

   (3) has blond hair

   (4) has unruly hair

10. The words *el platform, teeming, hostile city, big office buildings,* and *City Hall Station* suggest that the story takes place in

   (1) Miami

   (2) San Francisco

   (3) New York City

   (4) Dallas

Answer the questions in the space provided.

11. What four actions from the story show Mr. Lovides's compassion?

_____

_____

_____

12. What clue in paragraph 6 tells you that Joey is new to this country?

_____

_____

Check your answers on page 145.

WRITING WORKSHOP

Brainstorm: Find a Character

Think of someone you know well. Would he or she make a good character in a story?

Focus: List Characteristics

Note as many facts as you can think of about your character's life. List details about his or her physical appearance, emotions, personality, family, friends, job, and interests. Try to use similes, metaphors, and other forms of imagery in your descriptive notes. For example, "Lisa's eyes were as cold and shiny as pebbles in a northern stream."

Expand: Write a Description

Now that you know a lot about your character, write a paragraph or two describing him or her. Make sure to show what your character looks like. Also include details about what the character says, does, and thinks.

CHAPTER 13 | **SETTING**

Just as you picture characters in your mind, you also picture the setting of stories you read. The **setting** of a story is the time and place in which its events occur. For example, it might take place at the beach during the summer or in a hospital during the winter.

A story may be set in a real place or in a place the author made up. It may be set in the past, the present, or the future. Sometimes, you can tell what the setting is from the beginning of the story. But other times, you must infer the setting from the story's details.

Read the following paragraph. Look for information about the setting of this story.

Ohio Plowgirl

Lydia mopped her sweaty face with her handkerchief. She could see the heat rise up in waves from the cornfield. It was surprisingly hot for a spring day. And she had been plowing the field for hours. The horses that pulled the plow were tired, too. Lydia remembered the days when her biggest job was to cook for her father and brothers when they came in from planting. But two years ago the Civil War had started, and now it seemed all the men in Ohio were in the army. Lydia and her mother and her little sisters needed corn to eat and to feed the cows. To keep from starving, they had to do the work themselves.

■ Based on the passage, answer the following questions.

1. The paragraph gives a lot of information about this story's setting. Where does it take place?

_____

2. When does the story take place?

_____

3. During what season of the year does the story take place?

_____

4. Write the sentence that tells you this.

_____

5. Is the setting in this paragraph during the early morning or late afternoon?

_____

6. Write the sentence that helps you figure this out.

_____

7. The Civil War took place from 1861 to 1865. In what year does the story take place?

_____

8. Write the clue from the story that helps you to answer this question.

_____

1. in a cornfield in Ohio; 2. in the second year of the Civil War; 3. spring; 4. It was surprisingly hot for a spring day; 5. late afternoon; 6. And she had been plowing in the field for hours; 7. 1863; 8. Two years ago the Civil War had started.

STRATEGY: UNDERSTANDING SETTING

▶ Look for words that tell you where the story is set. Indoors or out? City or country? A real place or a made-up one?
▶ Look for words that tell you when the story takes place. What year? What season? What time of day?

Exercise

Read the story and complete the exercise that follows.

The term *ugly American* describes Americans in a foreign country whose behavior offends the people of that country. What do the people in this story think of the American tourists?

An American Twenty

by Pamela Hathaway Harrer

"I told you already I was listening, Miguel." Juana Carreras glanced down at her middle child. Shadows of laundry and leaves shifted over the bare dirt as a thick breeze moved behind the bark-walled house. Juana ran one hand through her sweat-dampened hair. Several chickens scratched just inside the doorway. Juana rested her hands on her hips as she stared at them. Only one egg today. She turned back to the wire and draped a girl's yellow dress, lightly bunched, between the barbs. Cool water dropped on Juana's feet.

"Mama, listen!" Miguel kicked up a small cloud of dust with his toes.

"Miguel, what?" She needed more water. Both ten-gallon cans were almost dry. Juana turned to her nine-year-old. "Your pants are filthy. Here, give them to me so Marta can wash them." Juana pulled a damp pair of shorts out of the tree beside her for her son to put on. A moment later, she threw his salt-stiff pants into a tin basin filled with soapy gray water several feet away. "Why are you back?"

"I'm telling you! I went to the . . ."

"You can get more water as long as you're here, then." Juana raised her voice as she turned toward the doorway. "Marta, I want you to wash the little ones now. Miguel is here to help you carry water."

The eldest, Marta, stepped out of the darkness nudging her four-year-old brother ahead of her with her knee. She held a **listless**[1] baby under her arm and pulled another slightly older one behind her. She struggled briefly to **disentangle**[2] the baby from her long ponytail before settling the children in the shade under a palm.

---

¹listless: tired, bored
²disentangle: to free from

Miguel tugged on the pocket of his mother's worn blue dress. "Mama, I went to the beach by the pink hotel today, the one that Papa helped to build, where the sand is soft . . ."

Juana batted his hand. "You didn't swim there . . ."

"I didn't. But I . . ."

"You swim on our side if you need water." Juana's voice was hard.

Miguel looked at the ground. "The rocks cut."

Juana crossed her arms over her broad chest. She remembered, before the hotels, sinking into the smooth wet sand, sifting it between her toes. Roberto's work on the pink one had fed them. She fed the children herself now, since Roberto had been killed in a construction accident on a site at the edge of town.

Miguel shifted his weight from foot to foot in the soft dust of the yard as Juana regarded him. She sighed. "There's no time for swimming on either side of the bay today, Miguel."

"But listen! I was the first boy down today, and I got the first tourists I saw to hire me."

Juana nodded. She had Miguel make only three trips to the well by the blue church for water in the morning, so he could get to the beach early. There weren't always enough tourists in the late summer for so many boys. Her two girls between him and Marta carried the rest of the water, before following him to the beach with baskets of mangoes and oranges to sell for three **Dominican pesos**[3] each.

Palms rustled as the heavy breeze changed directions. The sour smell of sewage drifted over them from the narrow flow at the edge of the road.

Miguel pulled again on his mother's skirt. "There were two of them, Mama, a man and a woman. Americanos, they said."

A drop of sweat rolled down Juana's neck. She was almost out of rice.

"The man went away in a boat with the fisherman, and . . ."

Juana looked at the sky. She'd woven another sheet of bark under the hole in the roof from the inside. Would it still leak?

". . . the lady stayed. She couldn't understand me, except a few words, but we made pictures in the sand to talk."

The goat, Lupita, strained against the rope that held her near the house. Juana reminded herself to have one of the children milk her later.

"It was too hot for the lady, so she went in the water all the time, and I stayed on the end of her chair with her bag while she was gone . . ."

---

³Dominican peso: standard of money used in the Dominican Republic

"You're a good boy, Miguel. Now Marta needs your help."

"Mama! She was gone for a long time once when she did the parachute behind the boat and . . ."

Juana slapped at a fly on her arm, then rested the back of her hand over her eyes. Waves crashed rhythmically against the rocks below the dump two roads away.

"Each time she came back I washed the sand off her feet with sea water from my bottle, and I put oil on her back . . ."

Marta made a path in the ground as she dragged a brown plastic basin through the dirt toward her mother. She stopped beside the laundry pile. One by one, she **retrieved**⁴ her **charges**⁵ from the spot where she'd propped them, and fit them into the small, high-sided tub. She emptied the last inch of water from the nearest can into the tub over the children, then replaced it in the dirt. She did the same with the second.

Juana's stomach burned. "Did you eat today, Miguel?"

"She got pizza and Coca-Cola from the hotel for me, and when she got sand in hers, she gave me that, too."

"Good." Juana reached down for a frayed, wet towel.

Marta scanned the yard. "There's no more water, Mama."

"Use that," Juana pointed with her bare foot toward the low tin basin nearby, "and Miguel is going to get you more. Don't use any more soap."

Marta lifted the basin with both hands. She staggered several steps, rested it on the edge of the tub, then flooded the children with laundry water. Miguel's shorts sunk between them.

"Mama," Miguel said, "she asked me if I went to school."

"School!" Juana shook her head. A gull screamed in the distance.

"The man came back, and he swam, too, and I washed his feet, too. Not the lady. I stayed on the end of her chair. She just closed her eyes, but she didn't go to sleep."

"Miguel, after you've gotten water, I need you to catch some of the chickens."

"As soon as the man went to sleep, she got up and went through her bag. She kept looking at the man, but he stayed asleep."

Juana noticed for the first time the fists he held tightly clenched against his chest.

---

⁴**retrieved:** got and brought back
⁵**charges:** those one takes care of

"She put her finger over her lips at me, and then . . ." Miguel slowly opened one hand, "she gave me this."

Juana took the balled-up paper. Her eyes widened as she gently flattened out the green bill. **Veinte.**[6] An American twenty. She held her breath as she stared at it, then in one motion exhaled and stuffed it into the pocket without the hole. Rice. Kerosene.

"The man woke up and when they left, he gave me this." Miguel handed his mother a ten-peso coin, from his other fist, that she slipped into the same pocket.

"You did well, Miguel. You keep them happy. Now go get water for your sister so I can finish hanging the wash." Juana's heart pounded as she turned back to the pile by her feet. A plane passed by overhead.

Miguel scooped two plastic water buckets from a pile next to the door. He leapt across the foul stream at the end of the road, then disappeared toward the well.

Juana carefully arranged a small shirt on the wire, imagining for a moment it was one of the stiff white shirts the children wear to school. She imagined hanging alongside it the dark navy pants school boys wear. Juana remembered the blue jumper she'd worn as a girl for two years, when her family could pay, before she was needed back at home. Juana always needed all of her children who were old enough to walk.

A baby cried out—Juana knew without looking it wasn't hers. She reached into her pocket to feel the paper again. Two hundred forty pesos on the black market. Medicine.

Miguel appeared shortly and gave the bottles to Marta, then stood back quietly watching as she sat each child on the edge of the tub. Marta poured the rinse water over them separately. Juana turned when the smallest whimpered and coughed. The older two giggled as they slipped back into the dirty water of the tub.

"Come here, Miguel," Juana called.

Miguel shuffled through crushed leaves and bits of bark to his mother.

Juana took him firmly by the shoulders. "What did you say to the lady when she asked you about school?"

"I told her, Mama, it costs too much money." Miguel grinned.

Juana held him tightly so he couldn't get away as she kissed his forehead. "You're a smart boy." She rotated him to face the doorway of their home. "Now go and kill the brown hen. The little ones will pull off the feathers after Marta is done."

. . . .

[6]**veinte:** twenty

Answer the questions in the space provided.

1. What time of the year does this story take place? _____

2. Is "An American Twenty" set in a real or an imaginary place?

   _____

3. Does this story take place in the United States? List clues that tell you where it takes place.

   _____

   _____

4. List five clues that tell you this story is set in a warm climate.

   _____

   _____

5. List five clues that tell you the Carreras family lives in poverty.

   _____

   _____

   _____

6. Does Miguel speak English? How do you know? _____

   _____

7. What clues tell you that one of the children is sick? _____

   _____

8. Did the woman tourist want the man to know that she had given Miguel the $20? How do you know?

   _____

   _____

9. Why doesn't Miguel go to school? _____

10. The author contrasts the world of the Carreras family with the world of the American tourists. Across from the words listed on the left, write descriptions from the story showing how the characters' worlds are different. **The first one is done for you.**

	Carreras family	**American tourists**
beach	rocky, dangerous	smooth, soft, sandy, safe
housing		
ways each spends time		
food		

Check your answers on page 146.

WRITING WORKSHOP

Brainstorm: Choose a Topic

Think about an event in your own life that reminds you of this story. Have you ever had a stroke of luck like Miguel's twenty-dollar bill? Has money or a job or a relationship turned up just when you needed it most? Choose one episode to write about.

Focus: Make Notes on the Setting

Picture in your mind the event you've chosen. When did it take place? What year was it? What season? What time of day? Where did it take place? Make some notes of what your surroundings were like.

Expand: Write a Paragraph

Write a paragraph describing the piece of luck you experienced. Use the details you've listed to bring the scene to life. Then ask a friend to read your paragraph. Was the setting clear enough to create a picture in his or her mind?

CHAPTER 14 | **PLOT**

If you describe to a friend the movie you saw last night, you'll probably spend most of your time describing its plot. The **plot** is the series of events in a story. It's the answer to the question "What's the story about?"

If Ricardo meets Emily, that's just an event. But suppose Ricardo meets Emily, falls in love with her, has a fight with her, and then wins her back. That's a plot. As you can tell from this example, plot depends on the characters we discussed in Chapter 12. Plot can't exist without people. The nature of the characters in the story will determine what actions they take. The purpose of a story's beginning is to introduce its characters.

Plot also depends on conflict, which we'll discuss in the next chapter. The plot focuses on a character's problem and the action he or she takes to solve that problem. The action of a good story builds to a turning point. The climax is the most exciting part of the story. It is when the character's problem is solved and we find out whether the person gets what he or she wants. Then the story ends with a believable conclusion.

Every plot has these four basic parts: a beginning, a problem, a climax, and a conclusion. These elements draw you into the story and make you want to know what will happen next.

The following two paragraphs sum up a plot. Here, it is boiled down to its basic parts. In a real story, it would be spread out over the whole length of the story. It would also be woven together with characters, setting, and conflict.

High School Flame

Eric and Beth dated all through high school. Then they had a fight about something silly and broke up. A few years later, he heard she'd gotten married. Eric's friends kept fixing him up with nice, attractive women, but it never worked out. He compared all the women to Beth.

A few years later, Eric was shopping at the supermarket when he saw Beth. She looked as beautiful as ever. When Eric spoke to Beth, she was friendly, but she seemed in a hurry. She said she had to take one of her kids to soccer practice and feed the other two. Maybe she's divorced, Eric thought. So he asked about her husband. "He's great. He's out of town for a few days, and I miss him so much! You'd think we were still teenagers. Remember how intense everything felt at that age?" Yeah, I remember, thought Eric. He said good-bye to Beth and took his one lonely pork chop to the checkout counter.

· ·

■ Based on the passage, answer the following questions.

This plot summary begins with a brief history of Eric and Beth's relationship as teenagers. The problem is that Eric, after many years, is still "carrying a torch" for Beth.

What do you think is the climax of this story?

_____

You're right if you said **when Eric runs into Beth at the supermarket**.

What is the conclusion, or end of the story?

_____

You're correct if you said **when Eric said good-bye to Beth and took his one lonely pork chop to the checkout counter**.

STRATEGY: IDENTIFYING PLOT

▶ At the beginning, make mental pictures of the characters.
▶ Notice the problem that the characters must solve.
▶ Identify the climax by asking "What is the most exciting point in the story? Where is the problem solved?"
▶ Determine whether the conclusion follows logically from the beginning, problem, and climax.

Exercise

Read the story and complete the exercise that follows.

Have you ever jumped to the wrong conclusion about someone? Was it because of the person's race or religion or looks? Have you ever been wrongly accused?

The Wallet

by R. Russell

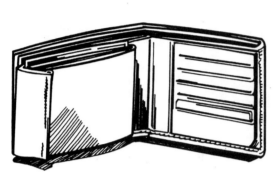

The guy was almost out the door of the train before Howard noticed he was missing his wallet. That did it. He thought he'd seen the guy edging up behind him just a minute before, and now he was sure. Without another thought, he sprang out of the subway in pursuit. The man saw him. He was a young black guy, slim, maybe as tall as Howard, certainly no taller than six and a half feet, and he began to sprint through the station toward the turnstiles for the east exit. Howard kept right behind him. All that handball was paying off.

The squealing of another train in the station and the hot breath of the tunnels were hounding them out toward the surface. If anybody thought it odd to see a balding, middle-aged white man the size and shape of a bear in a business suit running after a young black man, they certainly didn't let on. Of course, there were no cops around.

The guy cleared the turnstile in one leap, like a track star taking a hurdle, and bounded up the stairs to the street. Howard knew better than to try it, and lost valuable seconds climbing over the stile. No one tried to stop him. He charged up the grimy stairs, shouldering his way past a **clot**[1] of teenagers who shouted something at him as he emerged into the daylight.

The man was half a block away and still running. Howard clenched his teeth and ran harder. His necktie was hampering his breathing, but he couldn't take the time to stop and loosen it. Looking up, he saw that he was gaining on the man, slowly. He tried to note details so he could report them later. Physical characteristics: what would a cop want to know? About six feet tall, slim, hair cut close but not severely, dark pants, a blue baseball jacket, some sort of leather

---

¹clot: group

shoes—not sneakers. Obviously the guy hadn't expected to be followed. He was slowing down. He looked back at Howard with panic and kept running. Howard almost grinned, then thought about what he might have to do next. Jesus, what if the guy had a gun? or a knife? The hell with it; he could take him.

"The wallet!" he bellowed. He let the shouts come with his breathing, like a chant. "The wallet! The wallet! The wallet!"

The man glanced back over his shoulder again as he ran. He was visibly shaken. That's right, you son of a bitch, Howard thought. Here comes two hundred pounds of ex-wrestler. You messed with the wrong guy this time. "The wallet! The wallet! The wallet!"

Without breaking stride, the guy flung the wallet back at Howard and turned a corner, sprinting off down the block. Howard pounded to a stop, completely winded. He bent over the wallet on the sidewalk, his hands on his knees as he tried to catch his breath. He felt a little dizzy. Panting, he looked around him. Where was he? He hadn't even noticed what stop they'd gotten off at. Young foreign-looking men in strap T-shirts sat on the stoops of some of the buildings in small groups, watching him with a **leisurely**[2] hostility that made him shiver. Jesus, he thought, where the hell am I? Out of the frying pan, into the fire.

He picked up the wallet and jammed it into his suitcoat pocket. Still wheezing a little, he began to walk with what he hoped was a casual air. A small child passed him on the sidewalk, turning to stare at him as he passed. Howard tried to keep his eyes straight ahead, not inviting any challenges or further trouble. A huge white Cadillac with opaque tinted windows cruised slowly past, the grille of the car sneering at Howard as it slid by.

He buttoned his jacket and stopped himself from whistling. Someone shouted something **unintelligible**[3] behind him, maybe in Spanish?, but he ignored it. God, how far had they run? This street didn't look at all familiar. Then he spotted the subway entrance at the end of the next block, and a wave of relief washed over him like a drug. He knew he looked like a fool, some white businessman scurrying out of the ghetto with his tail between his legs, but he didn't care. By the time he reached the subway stairs, he was almost running again.

For the rest of the ride downtown Howard kept his hands tucked tightly under his armpits as if he were cold. No one was going to touch that wallet again. From his seat at the far end of the car, he glared suspiciously at the other passengers who milled about restlessly. Every one of them looked like a thief to him: three teenaged boys obviously skipping school, an old black man in soiled

---

[2]**leisurely:** unhurried
[3]**unintelligible:** unclear

workclothes with a tired scowl on his face, a thin young man in a jogging suit pretending to read a section of newspaper folded to the size of a sandwich. Howard was **deliberately**[4] maintaining a safe zone around him by jutting his elbows out and glaring at anyone who approached his seat. By the time he reached his stop downtown, his shoulders and neck ached, and his legs were tightening up from the unaccustomed running earlier. It was still only 9:30 in the morning, and he was exhausted.

As he walked into the office he felt like a soldier limping home from a long foreign campaign. The receptionist, Vicky, was on the phone and looked up as he came in. "Oh, wait, here he is now." She raised her eyebrows to catch his attention. "Howard, it's your wife on the line. I'll switch the call through to your office."

Howard plodded into his office, shut the door behind him, and collapsed into his chair behind the desk. For a moment he just sat there listening to the sound of his own breathing. Boy, wait until he told Lynn about this. She'd sure let him take the car in to work now. He picked up the phone.

"Hi, Hon." She sounded cheerful and hurried. "Don't have much time, I have to go pick Jeannette up at school. The nurse called and said she'd thrown up in class. I just wanted to let you know that you left your wallet on the kitchen table this morning."

. . . .

---

⁴deliberately: on purpose

PART A

Number the events of the story in the correct time order. One is done for you.

___ Howard takes the train back to his office.

_1_ Howard notices his wallet is missing.

___ Howard springs out of the subway in pursuit of the young black man.

___ The young man flings the wallet back at Howard.

___ Howard's wife calls to tell him he forgot his wallet at home.

___ Howard yells "The wallet!" at the young man as he chases him.

PART B

Circle the best answer for each question.

1. The first character you meet in the story is
   (1) Howard
   (2) the guy Howard thinks stole his wallet
   (3) Howard's wife
   (4) the driver of the white Cadillac

2. What problem is Howard trying to solve?
   (1) His wallet is missing.
   (2) He's late for work.
   (3) He's out of shape.
   (4) He doesn't have a car.

3. What wrong inference does Howard make?
   (1) The train is late.
   (2) His wife took his wallet.
   (3) The young black man stole his wallet.
   (4) The other passengers on the train are undercover cops.

4. What inference does the man Howard chases make?
   (1) Howard is a police officer.
   (2) Howard is trying to get his wallet.
   (3) The other passengers on the train are thieves.
   (4) He got off at the wrong stop.

5. What is the climax of the story?

   (1) when Howard begins chasing the other man

   (2) when the man throws his wallet at Howard

   (3) when Howard gets to the office

   (4) when Howard learns that his wallet is at home

6. What is the setting of the story?

   (1) a subway train

   (2) a city street

   (3) an office

   (4) all of the above

7. What effect does the apparent theft of his wallet have on Howard?

   (1) It makes him mad at his wife.

   (2) It brings on a heart attack.

   (3) It makes him suspicious of all the other passengers.

   (4) It leads him to quit his job.

8. What is Howard's physical description?

   (1) a balding, middle-aged white man

   (2) a two-hundred-pound ex-wrestler

   (3) a man wearing a business suit

   (4) all of the above

9. Which is part of the physical description of the man Howard chases?

   (1) long-haired

   (2) chubby

   (3) wearing leather shoes

   (4) short

10. Is the ending of "The Wallet" an effective one? Why or why don't you think so?

   _____

   _____

   _____

Check your answers on pages 146-147.

WRITING WORKSHOP

Brainstorm: Remember an Event

Think about a time in your life when you jumped to the wrong conclusion. Maybe you assumed the worst about someone because he or she was different from you. Or maybe you gave somebody too much credit because he or she was attractive. Remember the circumstances when this happened to you.

Focus: Describe Your Feelings

Recall how you felt when you misjudged this person. Make notes about those feelings. Did you feel foolish about drawing the wrong conclusion? Did you feel guilty or ashamed that you made a wrong judgment about the person? Did you feel disappointed in yourself when you realized you had made a mistake about the person?

Did you just try to put the event out of your mind and pretend it didn't happen? Or did you go back to the person to try to explain why you reacted to him or her as you did?

Expand: Write a Paragraph

Write a paragraph describing the event and the way it made you feel. When you found out you had been wrong, what did you do?

CHAPTER 15 | CONFLICT

When you hear the word *conflict*, you think of a fight. It doesn't have to mean that in fiction—although it can. In a story, **conflict** is the problem the characters are trying to solve. Conflict is what the plot depends on. As you learned in Chapter 14, the **plot** is a character's problem and the action he or she takes to solve the problem.

Conflict can be internal or external. **Internal conflict** is a struggle that takes place in one character's mind. The person may have to figure out what is the right thing to do and then decide whether to do it. An example is a child in a store who wants a toy. He has no money, but he also knows that stealing is wrong. Does he satisfy his urge or do the right thing? That's internal conflict.

External conflict is a struggle between one character and some outside force. That force might be another person or a sports team or a whole town. In a movie like *Star Wars*, external conflict is between the good guys and an entire universe. External conflict can also be a struggle against a force of nature, like an earthquake, a plane crash, or a fire in a skyscraper.

Whether internal or external, conflict is what makes the action of a story exciting. You read on because you want to find out who won. Conflict is introduced early in a story. Then it builds, and the reader's interest builds, too. Involving the reader by increasing conflict is called **suspense**. The peak of the conflict is the story's climax.

As you read the following passage, decide what conflict the main character faces. Notice the steps she takes to solve it. Would you handle the conflict in the same way Gloria does?

Harassed

One night Gloria's boss, Henry, asked her to work late. "I'm sorry, but I can't. I'm busy tonight," she said.

"But we have to finish these financial statements by tomorrow, and you're my best worker. Could you stay just until 6:00?" Henry asked.

Gloria agreed. At 5:00 her co-workers went home. Gloria stayed at her desk and continued checking figures. Then Henry came out of his office. "What a day," he said, rubbing his neck. "I need a massage."

"About this income statement," Gloria said quickly. "Isn't the decimal point in the wrong place?" She swiveled her computer screen to face Henry, but he moved it back and walked around behind her. He leaned over her shoulder. "You're right. That should be millions of dollars, not thousands. I told you I needed you." Henry began to rub Gloria's shoulders. "Feels like you need a massage, too. Relax."

Gloria froze. She wanted to roll her chair over his foot, but instead she said, "I really have to go now." She grabbed her purse and ran out the door.

. . . .

■ Based on the passage, answer the following questions.

With whom does Gloria have a conflict?

_____

If you said **her boss, Henry**, you are right.

What is the conflict about?

_____

You might say **it's about sexual harassment** or **a problem between Gloria and her boss**.

Is the conflict internal or external?

_____

This conflict is external, with another person. But it is also internal. Gloria may have trouble deciding how to handle Henry's advances.

> ### STRATEGY: IDENTIFYING CONFLICT
>
> ▶ Look for the problem the characters face.
> ▶ Decide whether the problem is internal or external.
> ▶ Identify the steps characters take to solve their problem.
> ▶ See if these steps lead to other problems.
> ▶ Ask yourself if you would solve the problem the same way.

Exercise

Read the story and complete the exercise that follows.

Getting involved with a married person can have disastrous effects. What type of phone call does the main character want to make?

232-9979

by Carol Edelstein

Maybe calling you was a mistake. I could hear the kids. I do not know how I will begin to admit to what I have done.

I suppose I will start by parking next to your house. But immediately I begin to imagine road construction that will make this impossible. I will find a place, though, even if it means the Quick Stop parking lot. This won't be any quick stop, though, if you are home, and answer my knock. I have nothing to say, but I think I'm going to need a lot of time to say it.

I don't know how far back I should go. There have been recent volcanic **eruptions**[1] on Venus. The newspaper said "recent," as defined by scientists, is "300,000 to several million" years ago. But I guess I'll start with three winters ago, December 19 to be exact, when your husband and I got into our first accident. Car accident. Nobody hurt, but addresses were exchanged, license plate numbers, insurance information—and I'll admit, I couldn't help it, I noted your husband's eye color. Hazel.

Nothing else would have happened between us if three weeks later I had not returned the box of **farina**[2] with flour-beetles to Bonno's Food Warehouse where I don't usually shop because of incidents like the above and also my ex-sister-in-law works there and we have never seen eye-to-eye. How could I have intended for your husband to be right ahead of me in the checkout, buying formula and plastic diapers? The first thing I noticed was his neck brace, but then, when I saw who he was, I had to inquire. If I was going to get smacked with a lawsuit I wanted to know about it. Wouldn't you?

---

¹eruptions: explosions
²farina: a kind of cereal

But even then nothing else might have happened if, on January 16, my downstairs neighbor Matty had not smoked in bed. I remember the date clearly because I had taken off work that morning to bring my mother in for a root canal. She turned out to be allergic to the ether or whatever it is they made her suck and she practically died in the chair.

I've lectured Matty about smoking safely in bed but she doesn't learn. She practically burned down the hallway, which needed it, but if it weren't for your husband and his men it could have gone further.

I was **unintentionally**³ in my yellow robe, kind of shivering, and I said, "Hank Henkins!" because by then I knew him by name.

"Hank Henkins! That can't be you!" Of course, I was pleased to see him under those circumstances—you would've been, too. And I'll admit it even if he doesn't—that's when I think he first noticed *my* eye color. Just for the record, they're blue.

This is the silly speech I am driving around with, although I have not yet made the call. I have Elly Henkins' number and I have driven by her house frequently enough to know she is home. The garage door is open, and the twins' stroller, in the middle of the sidewalk, is in a suggestive position. It is time to make a speech of some kind. I am over-my-head in love with Hank Henkins, and it won't wait until Kathy and Pam are grown up. It won't even wait until they are at least prom age, which Hank and me were both trying for. I thought we could have the longest flirt in history with no **dire**⁴ consequences, but now a thing has happened and I can't wait.

· ·

PART A
Answer the questions in the space provided.

1. What is the first thing the narrator thinks about when she sees Hank at the warehouse?

_____

2. What clues tell you where the narrator lives?

_____

_____

---

³**unintentionally:** not on purpose
⁴**dire:** disastrous

3. Why do you think Kathy and Pam are mentioned?

_____

_____

4. How does Hank's job involve him with the narrator?

_____

_____

5. What does the narrator want to tell Hank's wife?

_____

_____

PART B

Circle the best answer for each question.

1. What is the main conflict in this story?
   (1) The narrator's house burned down.
   (2) The narrator's mother almost died at the dentist's.
   (3) The narrator is in love with another woman's husband.
   (4) The narrator was in a car accident.

2. What internal conflict does the narrator face?
   (1) She feels guilty about trying to break up a family.
   (2) She feels angry with her neighbor for starting the fire.
   (3) She feels jealous of Elly Henkins for having children.
   (4) She feels like getting out of this relationship.

3. How does the narrator plan to handle her conflict with Elly Henkins?
   (1) She plans to make Hank leave his wife.
   (2) She plans to tell Elly about her affair with Hank.
   (3) She plans to make Elly hate Hank so she'll leave him.
   (4) She plans to kill Elly.

4. What physical description of the main character do we have?
   (1) She has blue eyes.
   (2) She has blond hair.
   (3) She is short and round.
   (4) She's wearing a neck brace.

5. What word best describes the main character's state of mind right now?

   (1) happy

   (2) jealous

   (3) frightened

   (4) confused

6. What is the setting of this story?

   (1) inside a convenience store

   (2) in a telephone booth

   (3) in the Henkinses' neighborhood

   (4) in the Henkinses' garage

Check your answers on page 147.

WRITING WORKSHOP

Brainstorm: Find a Topic

Think about some conflicts in your life. We all have many conflicts, both internal and external. For example, maybe you're juggling your job and child care and housework. If so, you have the conflict of not enough time. You may also have an external conflict with your spouse about who's responsible for what. And you may have an internal conflict because you don't feel you're doing a good enough job as a parent. Make a list of some of the conflicts you face.

Focus: Write Down Details

Choose one conflict to write about. Make notes on how this conflict makes you feel. If it's an external conflict, write down conversations you've had (or imagined having) with the other people involved.

Expand: Write a Short Story

Take your conflict and turn it into a story. That means you can solve it in a way you couldn't in real life. You can make the other people say and do whatever you want them to. Giving the main character a name other than your own may help remind you that this is fiction, not fact. Remember to describe your characters and your setting. Figure out what the climax of your story will be.

CHAPTER 16 | THEME AND MAIN IDEA

Writers often use specific characters and events to make statements about life in general. A message about life or human nature is called the **theme** of a story. The theme is the **main idea** of the story. Often, a story's theme can be interpreted in more than one way.

We all tend to draw conclusions about life in general based on our specific experiences. For example, if you often read in the newspaper about criminals getting caught, you may conclude that crime does not pay. If your co-worker gets a raise and you don't, you may conclude that life is not fair. If you read about a movie star's painful divorce, you may conclude that money can't buy love. All of these conclusions could be used as the themes of short stories.

For more examples, look at the stories you've read so far in this unit. The theme of "The Eyes of Mr. Lovides" is that our impressions about other people can sometimes be mistaken. Mr. Lovides was not as Joey thought him to be. The theme of "The Wallet" is that it's dangerous to jump to conclusions without knowing the facts. The theme of "An American Twenty" is that money exercises a powerful influence over people's lives. The theme of "232-9979" is that getting involved with a married person can have disastrous effects.

Usually you have to infer the theme of a story. To do this, think about the details and decide what main idea connects them. Ask yourself, "What lesson about life did I learn from this story?"

■ As you read the following passage, try to figure out the theme.

Just Rewards

George blew on his hands and pulled the cardboard up to his chin. He had been sleeping on the corner of Elm and Oak for a week now. He was getting used to never taking a shower and never getting enough to eat. But how would he get used to freezing, now that winter was here? He'd just have to get up and move around. He walked over to the appliance store on Fourth Street, where they left the TVs on all night. George watched in a daze of hunger and tiredness. Suddenly, he recognized a face on the news. It was Martin Murk, his old boss.

Murk had owned an investment firm that cheated thousands of old people out of their life savings. Murk had gone to jail for five years. His company had folded, and George had found himself out of a job. He had drifted for a while, finding a few weeks of work here and there. His last job had been washing dishes in a restaurant. They let him go because business was so bad, and that's when he wound up on the street. Now he watched in disbelief as his thief of a boss was released from jail after only ten months. George heard the words "time off for good behavior . . . model prisoner . . . community service." Then the reporter said, "Mr. Murk will be returning to the finance industry as a partner in Sloane Investment Co." George shook his head and shuffled back to his spot on the pavement. It was over a heating vent, so he didn't want to lose it.

. . . .

■ Based on the passage, answer the following question.

What are some of the truths about life this story describes? List them.

_____

_____

_____

You might have said **it shows that homelessness is often a result of bad breaks, not something a person deserves**. Or you might have said **life is not fair** or **justice is only for the rich**. The theme may be expressed in different words.

STRATEGY: IDENTIFYING THEME/MAIN IDEA

▶ Decide what lessons the characters learn about life and about themselves.
▶ Ask yourself, "What did I learn from this story?"
▶ Put the author's message in your own words.

Exercise

Read the story and complete the exercise that follows.

Sometimes we have to sacrifice our own desires for the good of someone or something else. What drives Noni to make the choice he makes?

Two Were Left

by Hugh B. Cave

On the third night of hunger, Noni thought of the dog. Nothing of flesh and blood lived upon the floating ice island with its towering berg except those two.

In the breakup, Noni had lost his sled, his food, his furs, even his knife. He had saved only Nimuk, his great devoted husky dog. And now the two, **marooned**[1] on the ice, eyed each other **warily**[2]—each keeping his distance.

Noni's love for Nimuk was real, very real—as real as hunger and cold nights and the gnawing pain of his injured leg in its homemade brace. But the men of his village killed their dogs when food was scarce, didn't they? And without thinking twice about it.

And Nimuk, he told himself, when hungry enough would seek food. "One of us will soon be eating the other," Noni thought. "So . . ."

He could not kill the dog with his bare hands. Nimuk was powerful, and much fresher than he. A weapon, then, was essential.

Removing his mittens, he unstrapped the brace from his leg. When he had hurt his leg a few weeks before, he had fashioned the brace from bits of harness and two thin strips of iron.

Kneeling now, he wedged one of the iron strips into a crack in the ice, and began to rub the other against it with firm, slow strokes.

Nimuk watched him intently, and it seemed to Noni that the dog's eyes glowed more brightly as night **waned**.[3]

1marooned: stranded, stuck
2warily: suspiciously
3waned: lessened

He worked on, trying not to remember why. The slab of iron had an edge now. It had begun to take shape. Daylight found his task completed.

Noni pulled the finished knife from the ice and thumbed its edge. The sun's glare, reflected from it, stabbed at his eyes and momentarily blinded him.

Noni steeled himself.

"Here, Nimuk!" he called softly.

The dog suspiciously watched him.

"Come here," Noni called.

Nimuk came closer. Noni read fear in the animal's gaze. He read hunger and suffering in the dog's labored breathing and awkward, dragging crouch. His heart wept. He hated himself and fought against it. Closer Nimuk came, wary of his intentions. Now Noni felt a thickening in his throat. He saw the dog's eyes and they were wells of suffering.

Now! Now was the time to strike!

A great sob shook Noni's kneeling body. He cursed the knife. He swayed blindly, flung the weapon far from him. With empty hands outstretched he stumbled toward the dog, and fell.

The dog growled **ominously**[4] as he warily circled the boy's body. And now Noni was sick with fear.

In flinging away the knife, he had left himself defenseless. He was too weak to crawl after it now. He was at Nimuk's mercy, and Nimuk was hungry.

The dog had circled him and was creeping up from behind. Noni heard the rattle of saliva in the savage throat.

He shut his eyes, praying that the attack might be swift. He felt the dog's feet against his leg, the hot rush of Nimuk's breath against his neck. A scream gathered in the boy's throat.

Then he felt the dog's hot tongue caressing his face.

Noni's eyes opened, **incredulously**[5] staring. Crying softly, he thrust out an arm and drew the dog's head down against his own. . . .

The plane came out of the south an hour later. Its pilot, a young man of the coast patrol, looked down and saw the large floating **floe**,[6] with the berg rising from its center. And he saw something flashing.

---

[4]**ominously:** warningly, dangerously
[5]**incredulously:** disbelievingly
[6]**floe:** large sheet of ice

It was the sun gleaming on something shiny, which moved. His curiosity aroused, the pilot banked his ship and descended, circling the floe. Now he saw, in the shadow of the peak of ice, a dark, still shape that appeared to be human. Or were there two shapes?

He set his ship down in a water lane and investigated. There were two shapes, boy and dog. The boy was unconscious but alive. The dog whined feebly but was too weak to move.

The gleaming object which had trapped the pilot's attention was a crudely fashioned knife, stuck point first into the ice a little distance away, and quivering in the wind.

. . . .

PART A
Circle *T* if the statement is true or *F* if it is false.

T F **1.** Noni thinks his only hope of survival is to kill his dog.

T F **2.** Nimuk wants to kill Noni.

T F **3.** Noni plans to kill Nimuk with his bare hands.

T F **4.** Noni and Nimuk are rescued because someone sees the unused knife.

T F **5.** The theme is that nature is cruel, and you must kill or be killed.

T F **6.** The theme is the conflict between a person's love for someone else and the instinct to survive.

T F **7.** Noni has an internal conflict.

T F **8.** Noni has a conflict with the pilot.

T F **9.** Noni has a conflict with nature.

T F **10.** The setting of the story is a city in Oregon.

T F **11.** The story takes place 200 years ago.

T F **12.** Noni is a compassionate character.

T F **13.** Noni is a selfish character.

T F **14.** Nimuk is a vicious dog.

T F **15.** Both Noni and Nimuk would have died if the pilot hadn't found them.

PART B

Answer the questions in the space provided.

1. Who shows compassion first, Noni or Nimuk?

   _____

2. How does the author switch the usual roles of man and beast?

   _____

3. When Noni hears the dog creeping up on him from behind, what does he think Nimuk is going to do? What does Nimuk actually do?

   _____

4. What makes the pilot take a closer look at the ice floe where Noni and Nimuk are stranded?

   _____

5. When Noni sharpens the piece of iron into a knife, the author says, "He worked on, trying not to remember why." What doesn't Noni want to remember?

   _____

Check your answers on pages 147-148.

WRITING WORKSHOP

Brainstorm: Find a Topic

The theme of "Two Were Left" is selflessness. Noni is ready to sacrifice his life for his dog. Think of a situation in which you had to sacrifice your own needs for someone or something else.

Focus: Write Down Details

Make notes about the situation in which you had to make a choice. Who was the other person or persons involved?

Expand: Write a Paragraph

Write one or several paragraphs describing your difficult choice. What general truth about life or human nature will your readers learn from your story?

Unit 4
REVIEW

Read the story and complete the exercise that follows.

People who are used to one way of life often have problems adjusting to a different one. How does life in a big city differ from life in the mountains?

Appalachian Home

by Lorraine Tolliver

I finish buttoning my blouse and run out to tell Daddy I'm ready. He is standing with one leg up on a three-foot wall in front of the rooming house, talking to a skinny little man with a face nearly as yellow as his hair.

"It's time for me to go," I say.

Daddy turns to walk the eight dirty blocks with me to my work before he goes to his insurance clerk's job.

I look at the mailboxes, trash bins, concrete and bricks. I miss the grass and trees of my Appalachian home and singing with my friends on the way to school.

These crowds on the Chicago streets look like they're play-acting their parts of leading grim, important lives. Their set faces are hard for me to take seriously. All the locked-in living by car, buses, traffic lights, business clothes, eight-hour time slots—it all seems like make-believe—earnest and weighty.

The way of the birds and horses and people in the mountains at home seems more real and easier and nicer. They live mostly in a house prettier than these people can build. It's got the sky for a ceiling and trees for walls and rocks and flowers for a carpet. It's usually on a mountaintop.

"Be a bum or be rich," Daddy says suddenly. "Nothing in-between."

I look at him and notice his eyes look like little patches of blue sky that have floated down.

I like what he said.

It's sort of close to what I was thinking.

It's about reaching.

Reaching for a place to see out from—a place where the air gives out and won't support the weight, where a few slip on through anyway . . .

It's what lies behind the crack of lightning in the deep sky over my Kentucky mountain home that caused me to ask, "What's back there?"

I've watched its mystery since my baby legs toddled onto Grandma's porch and later ran through the sprinkling rain to the white paling fence when they got a little stronger.

Now I know the moment again today when the curly-haired, pleasant-faced woman sits on the stool across from me at the counter of the downtown drugstore. She has threadlike wrinkles around her eyes. They make me think she laughs and cries a lot.

"My name is Beth. I'm thirty-seven. How old are you?"

"Sixteen," I say.

I have come here every morning for three weeks except Mondays to walk on these strange open slats in my cut-off sandals and queer drab tan dress and apron. I am a stranger to myself in it and put it on with awkward moves the way a French person might put on an Indian's **garb**.[1] I remember Mrs. Taylor, our high school English teacher, and how **alien**[2] she seemed to feel when we begged her till she tried to play boogie woogie on the piano.

"You don't like to work here?"

The woman's soft eyes brush my face, which must look as troubled as muddy water. I wipe dripped ice cream off the half-greasy counter with a damp cloth and smell the stale odor of sandwiches and soup. I think of putting food in front of people like feeding cows or pigs or sheep. I know I'm in a foreign place. I've stepped into some other way of being, and I hate it.

"No, I don't."

I do keep knowing how to say what I mean.

"Why are you here?" She folds her napkin into a little square. I don't want to tell her about my world, but she keeps looking at me. I finally answer her.

"I have to help Daddy buy a house in Kentucky. We're moving out of the mountains to the Blue Grass."

"He's here too?"

I'm tired. I've been tired for three weeks. I'm not used to standing for eight hours or lifting trays. I'm used to a quiet walk through the woods to school and having only people I trust around me. Mostly relatives. I'm used to walking in my uncle's house and smelling musky rose odor and looking up at his leather-bound books. I'm used to dreaming big dreams while I listen to the leaves crunch under my feet on my way to a new mountaintop where I can see something far. I'm used to listening to music float in from Cincinnati which sounds like it's been written by somebody better than anybody on the earth, and makes my feet want to lift my body up in the air to follow it.

---

¹garb: clothing
²alien: strange

My sister says, "Mom, make her stop."

But Mom says, "Let her dance if she wants to."

Daddy says we're poor, and I know we are. Back home I don't have nice clothes or even lunch money for school sometimes. If Daddy and I can work the whole summer here, he says that between the two of us and my older sister Elizabeth working at home for the county, we'll have enough money to put down on a house with lots of rooms in the Blue Grass. That's what he talks about all the time.

Only I'm so tired. And I have to learn what all these milk shakes and sodas cost, and I don't want to know. And I don't care that sandwiches get cold before ladies and their whiny children get them. That's what I told the customer yesterday just before I cried.

"I could tell the manager, you know," she said.

"I don't care whether you tell him or not," I said.

She didn't answer me, but she didn't tell him, either.

"Your father is here, too?" the pleasant-faced woman asks again.

"Yes." I am tired of her questions and my embarrassing answers. "Do you work?"

"Yes, I'm an artist."

That's when the lightning cracks and lets in a glimpse of what lies behind the sky. It hurts a person's eyes to even think of it.

"What kind?"

Artist. Any artist. That word is magic. That means things that make my bones melt and fly around in the sky. This woman is not a *person*-person like the bodies in the streets. This woman stands for big places—mystery places. Moving on.

"I paint. People's portraits, mostly. Come to my studio sometime, and I'll paint yours."

But I am too shy for that, I know.

"What do you want to be?" Thunder rolls off her question.

"Be a writer."

This is sort of news to me. Some feelings I haven't caught up with yet. It's got to do with that word "artist" and the crack of lightning.

What's back there—behind those blue-gold-silver streaks? People have followed out there—into a creation land they couldn't even imagine before. There it was, opening up and glowing and leading a person on into deeper and deeper places where, if a person could anyway write it down a little, or paint a hint of it, or plant it on the wind in music . . . Well, it was a trip worth taking—as long as a person was living on the earth anyway.

It was as close to God as anybody would get, and it was a little way of being God—on the lower spirals of a great ring of shaping mystery into solid stuff on the becoming wheel.

"Better go back to school. You don't need a house in the Blue Grass. Do you like school?" I think how she doesn't mention my southern accent the way other people here in Chicago do.

"Yes." School sounds happy and free, surrounded by green fields and stretching forever into places to see and imagine.

I go to the kitchen. I see stacks of wet, glistening glasses. I see that fat, bossy waitress Ellen with big bumps for breasts. She's about my mother's age. But Mom is pretty and wears soft blue to match her eyes. She never raises her voice, and when she laughs, she sounds like a bird singing to me. Mom is always kind and gentle and treats me like I'm a person. Who does this big woman think she is to tell me to fill up the salt shakers just to show me I have to do what she says?

In my mind I see a picture of *The Man with a Hoe* that used to hang in our history classroom. Here in the kitchen I recognize an echo of the pain on his worn-out face. I look at the sad lines marking the dried skin of the old man passing dirty bowls over a twirling wet brush standing in the middle of a sink of water. A fat boy waits beside him with round wads looking plastered like shields on his face and chin. His eyes are nearly hidden. Ellen's face looks as if the air has pushed against it so long and hard that all the soft parts are gone, and the nose and bones stick out sharp and set.

"I quit," I say suddenly without knowing about it ahead of time. I take off the strange clothes behind a screen. I throw the sandals in the corner.

"Why?" Ellen lifts her painted-on eyebrows.

"Because I don't like this place. I don't like you, either."

I look at the empty stool where the pleasant-faced woman had been sitting as I leave. I walk out the front glass doors. I am looking hard at the people and cars on the streets. I feel happy and free, but I am afraid about the Blue Grass house and about telling Daddy.

He just says, "Let's go home," and I know then that he knows, too, that our mountain home is better. I know I am like him. He carries his pen and notebook around all the time and sends off stories about the mountain people to newspapers. He kicks at the wind anytime he feels like it. That way he loses a lot of jobs. But I don't think he cares.

His way leaves time to study about how to break open the lightning chink and get back behind there where the light is too bright to see with just plain eyes.

. . . .

Circle the best answer for each question.

1. What have you learned about the main character?
   (1) She's homesick.
   (2) She's sixteen years old.
   (3) She wants to be a writer.
   (4) all of the above

2. Why did the main character's father move to Chicago?
   (1) He likes cities better than the country.
   (2) He wants to earn enough money for a house.
   (3) He paints portraits, and he's looking for new subjects.
   (4) He's running away from his family.

3. What can the main character tell about Beth from the lines around her eyes?
   (1) She laughs and cries a lot.
   (2) She's very old.
   (3) She's not very friendly.
   (4) She hates city life.

4. What is the setting of the story?
   (1) the mountains of Appalachia
   (2) Kentucky Blue Grass country
   (3) a drugstore snack counter in Chicago
   (4) a high-school classroom

5. What is the climax of the story?
   (1) when the main character meets Beth
   (2) when the main character quits her job
   (3) when the main character's father says, "Let's go home."
   (4) when the main character daydreams about home

6. With whom does the main character have an external conflict?
   (1) her father
   (2) her mother
   (3) Beth
   (4) Ellen

7. What is the main character's internal conflict?

    (1) She wants to be back home, but she needs to earn money.

    (2) She wants to be a writer, but she's afraid there's no future in it.

    (3) She hates her father, but she also needs him.

    (4) She has more money than she knows what to do with.

8. What is the theme of the story?

    (1) Love of money is the root of all evil.

    (2) There's no place like home.

    (3) Children should be seen but not heard.

    (4) Too many cooks spoil the broth.

9. What do you think the main character means when she says, "Artist. That means things that make my bones melt and fly around in the sky"?

    (1) She would faint if she had to pose for one of Beth's portraits.

    (2) She wants to be an airplane pilot.

    (3) She thinks that being an artist is magical and creative.

    (4) She's expecting it to rain.

10. The main character is like Joey in "The Eyes of Mr. Lovides" in that

    (1) she works in a diner

    (2) she has moved to a new and different place

    (3) she's often lonely and uncomfortable here

    (4) all of the above

11. The main character in "Appalachian Home" is different from Joey in "The Eyes of Mr. Lovides" in that

    (1) she's from Puerto Rico

    (2) she's all alone in the world

    (3) she decides to go home

    (4) she wouldn't do anything to risk her job

Check your answers on page 148.

POST-TEST

The Post-Test will help you check how well you have learned the reading skills in this book. You should take the Post-Test after you have completed all of the exercises in this book.

Read the passage and answer the questions that follow.

Do you sometimes have trouble sleeping? What can you do to help solve this problem?

Desperately Seeking Sleep

You've had a rough day, the kind you see in headache commercials. You come home and eat a big dinner. Then you feel the need for a nap. You need a cup of coffee to drag you off the couch. At bedtime, you toss and turn for hours. Every time you doze off, a car alarm sounds, or your spouse snores, or your neighbors crank up their stereo. Finally, you drift off, but minutes later the alarm drags you back from sleep.

What can you do? Don't panic. Most people spend close to one-third of their lives asleep (eight hours out of each twenty-four), so it's worth breaking bad habits to improve your quality of sleep. First, a big meal keeps you up at night. So does an empty stomach. Eat sensibly. Second, instead of a nap, fight that tired feeling with exercise. You'll get more done in the evening and you'll be ready to sleep when you get into bed. Third, knock off the caffeine, especially in the evening.

Noise at night is a problem, especially if you live in a city. Try earplugs. Develop a routine. Do the same things in the same order each night before bed, until falling asleep becomes part of the habit. And try to go to bed at the same time every night, even on weekends.

1. What is the main idea of this passage?
   (1) Life is exhausting.
   (2) There are things you can do to sleep better.
   (3) Caffeine will kill you.
   (4) You should go to bed at the same time every night.

2. Which would be a good title for this passage?
   (1) Wake Up and Smell the Coffee
   (2) Sleep Problems Are Leading Cause of Crime
   (3) Never Marry a Snorer
   (4) How to Get a Good Night's Sleep

3. What can you do to help you sleep?
   (1) Eat a sensible dinner.
   (2) Get enough exercise.
   (3) Develop a routine.
   (4) all of the above

4. How many hours a night does the average person sleep?
   (1) six
   (2) seven
   (3) eight
   (4) nine

5. What should you do if you feel tired hours before bedtime?

   _____

6. What substance should you avoid before bedtime?

   _____

Read the passage and answer the questions that follow.

Do you think jobs that hurt the environment should be cut? Or is it more important that people keep their jobs regardless of how they affect the environment?

Commentary: Jobs Versus the Environment

A lot of businesspeople work against programs that protect the environment. They believe protecting nature means losing jobs that people need to feed their families. If you save the forests of Oregon so spotted owls will have a place to live, then the loggers who cut down forests will be out of work. If you don't let tuna fishers use nets that kill dolphins, they can't catch enough tuna to make a living. If you make businesses pay for devices that clean the air in their smokestacks, they won't have enough money left to pay their workers.

But is this true? The evidence is that the choices are more complicated. For example, if Oregon's old forests are cut down, the loggers will be out of jobs soon anyway. And trees hundreds of years old will be gone forever. Cutting would not only destroy the spotted owls. It would also depress the economy, because fewer tourists would visit the state.

The same fishers who are killing dolphins are wiping out the tuna population. If they continue to overfish at the current rate, soon there won't be enough tuna left in the sea to support them. I believe most of the businesses that complain about how expensive it is to clean the air and water can afford it. And how can you put a price on giving children a world that won't poison them?

—Maria Gómez

7. Why do some businesspeople say we can't save the environment?

    (1) Saving it would mean losing a lot of jobs.

    (2) They can afford to live in clean, climate-controlled houses.

    (3) Spotted owls don't contribute anything to the world.

    (4) Pollution is just an imaginary problem.

8. Why would cutting down the old forests in Oregon be bad for everyone?

    (1) Trees hundreds of years old would be lost forever.

    (2) The loggers would soon be out of work.

    (3) The state would earn less money from tourists.

    (4) all of the above

9. Which of the following statements is a fact?

    (1) Protecting nature means losing jobs.

    (2) Most businesses can afford to clean the air they use.

    (3) Spotted owls live in the forests of Oregon.

    (4) You can't put a price on giving children a world that won't poison them.

10. Which of the following statements is an opinion?

    (1) It costs money to fight pollution.

    (2) Protecting nature means losing jobs.

    (3) Many of the trees in Oregon's forests are hundreds of years old.

    (4) all of the above

11. What clues in the commentary show a bias in favor of protecting the environment?

    (1) If they (fishers) continue to overfish at the current rate, soon there won't be enough tuna left in the sea to support them.

    (2) I believe most of the businesses that complain about how expensive it is to clean the air and water can afford it.

    (3) And how can you put a price on giving children a world that won't poison them?

    (4) all of the above

12. How many points of view are described in this commentary? _____

Read the cartoon and answer the questions that follow.

Did you ever get a reaction from someone that was different from what you expected?

13. What sport is the man watching on television? How do you know?

_____

_____

14. The born loser rushes to tell his wife about the game because
    (1) he wants her to calm him down
    (2) he wants her to share his excitement
    (3) he knows she'll be fascinated
    (4) he's too upset for words

15. What can you infer about Gladys's attitude toward baseball?
    (1) She's a real fan.
    (2) She prefers basketball.
    (3) She's supportive of her husband's interest in it.
    (4) She finds it boring.

16. Gladys's reaction makes her husband feel
    (1) let down
    (2) relieved
    (3) excited
    (4) furious

Read the poem and answer the questions that follow.

Have you ever wanted time to stand still?

The Night Will Never Stay

The night will never stay,
The night will still go by,
Though with a million stars
You pin it to the sky.

5   Though you bind it with the blowing wind
And buckle it with the moon,
The night will slip away
Like sorrow or a tune.

—by Eleanor Farjeon

17. How many verses does this poem have? _____

18. What idea does the author want to suggest in the poem?

_____

19. What are the pairs of words that rhyme in this poem?

_____

20. What is the rhyme pattern of this poem? _____

21. Is the poet trying for a mysterious or a funny tone? _____

22. What image does the poet use in the first verse?

_____

23. What sense does the last line of the poem appeal to? _____

24. What does the poet say the night is like when it slips away?

_____

25. Is the comparison in the last two lines a simile or a metaphor? _____

Read the passage and answer the questions that follow.

Has your life turned out as you wished? Have you done the things you really wanted to do?

A Man Told Me the Story of His Life

by Grace Paley

Vicente said: I wanted to be a doctor. I wanted to be a doctor with my whole heart.

I learned every bone, every organ in the body. What is it for? Why does it work?

The school said to me: Vicente, be an engineer. That would be good. You understand mathematics.

I said to the school: I want to be a doctor. I already know how the organs connect. When something goes wrong, I'll understand how to make repairs.

The school said: Vicente, you will really be an excellent engineer. You show on all the tests what a good engineer you will be. It doesn't show whether you'll be a good doctor.

I said: Oh, I long to be a doctor. I nearly cried. I was seventeen. I said: But perhaps you're right. You're the teacher. You're the principal. I know I'm young.

The school said: And besides, you're going into the army.

And then I was made a cook. I prepared food for two thousand men.

Now you see me. I have a good job. I have three children. This is my wife, Consuela. Did you know I saved her life?

Look, she suffered pain. The doctor said: What is this? Are you tired? Have you had too much company? How many children? Rest overnight, then tomorrow we'll make tests.

The next morning I called the doctor. I said: She must be operated immediately. I have looked in the book. I see where her pain is. I understand what the pressure is, where it comes from. I see clearly the organ that is making trouble.

The doctor made a test. He said: She must be operated at once. He said to me: Vicente, how did you know?

26. What does the test *not* show about Vicente?

    (1) He's good at math.

    (2) He would be a good engineer.

    (3) He would be a good doctor.

    (4) all of the above

27. Why does Vicente agree to the job the teachers want for him?

    (1) He figures they're older and wiser than he is.

    (2) He wants to stay out of the army.

    (3) He faints at the sight of blood.

    (4) He has three children to support.

28. List at least three clues that tell you Vicente would be a good doctor.

    _____

    _____

29. Over what period of time does this story take place?

    (1) less than one day

    (2) one week

    (3) ten days

    (4) at least ten years

30. What is the setting at the end of the story?

    (1) the school

    (2) the army

    (3) the doctor's office

    (4) none of the above

31. How did Vicente know what was wrong with his wife?

    (1) He looked it up in medical books.

    (2) He remembered what he had studied about the human body as a teenager.

    (3) He knew where the pain came from.

    (4) all of the above

32. What is the climax of this story?

    (1) when the tests say Vicente should be an engineer

    (2) when Consuela gets sick

    (3) when Vicente figures out what's wrong with Consuela

    (4) when Vicente learns every bone and organ in the body

Continued

33. Do you think Vicente's ethnic background could have anything to do with the advice the school gives him? If so, how?

_____

_____

34. When the doctor first examines Consuela, what does he think is wrong with her? What clues tell you?

_____

_____

35. With whom does Vicente have a conflict at the beginning of the story? What is the conflict?

_____

_____

36. Which statement best describes the theme of this story?
   (1) A good job is hard to find.
   (2) Do with your life what you think is right for you, not what other people tell you.
   (3) It's wise to marry a man who has studied medicine.
   (4) Knowing how something works is not the same as being able to fix it.

Check your answers on page 140.

POST-TEST EVALUATION CHART

Use the answer key on page 140 to check your answers to the Post-Test. Then find the item number of each question you missed and circle it on the chart below. Next, write the number of correct answers you had for each skill. If you need more practice in any skill, refer back to the chapter that covers that skill area.

Chapter	Skill	Item Numbers	Number Correct
1	Main idea	1, 2	——
2	Finding details	3, 4	——
3	Time order	5, 6	——
4	Main idea and Reasons	7, 8	——
5	Facts and Opinions	9, 10	——
6	Detecting bias	11, 12	——
7	Inferences	13, 14, 15, 16	——
8	Form	17, 18	——
9	Rhyme and Rhythm	19, 20	——
10	Imagery	21, 22, 23	——
11	Simile and Metaphor	24, 25	——
12	Character	26, 27, 28	——
13	Setting	29, 30	——
14	Plot	31, 32, 33	——
15	Conflict	34, 35	——
16	Theme and Main idea	36	——

POST-TEST ANSWER KEY

1. **(2)** The entire passage explains how a person can sleep better. Choices **(1)** and **(3)** overstate the facts. Choice **(4)** is true, but it is not the main idea.

2. **(4)** Choices **(1)** and **(2)** are not covered in the passage. While choice **(3)** (snoring) is mentioned, it is only a detail of the passage.

3. **(4)** All three choices are suggested in the passage.

4. **(3)** The average person sleeps about eight hours (paragraph 2, sentence 3).

5. Get some exercise instead of a nap (paragraph 2, sentence 7).

6. caffeine (paragraph 2, last sentence)

7. **(1)** Choices **(2)** and **(3)** may be true, but they are not mentioned in the passage. Choice **(4)** is not true.

8. **(4)** All three statements are mentioned in the commentary.

9. **(3)** Choices **(1)**, **(2)**, and **(4)** are opinions.

10. **(2)** Choices **(1)** and **(3)** are facts.

11. **(4)** All three statements are made as arguments in favor of protecting the environment.

12. Two points of view are described: first the pro-business viewpoint and then the pro-environment one.

13. baseball. The announcer refers to pitching and to runs, hits, walks, and errors.

14. **(2)** The details of the cartoon show that he is excited and wants his wife to share in it.

15. **(4)** The wife's boredom is shown in panel 5. Choices **(1)** and **(3)** can't be inferred from the cartoon, and choice **(2)** is not addressed.

16. **(1)** He is not as excited as he was before. The facts in the cartoon do not indicate that he is relieved, excited, or furious.

17. two verses

18. The title, "The Night Will Never Stay," suggests the fleetingness of time.

19. stay/away, by/sky, moon/tune

20. Lines 2 and 4 and lines 6 and 8, rhyme.

21. The poet is trying for a mysterious tone in the poem.

22. pinning the night to the sky with a million stars

23. hearing (slipping away like a tune)

24. sorrow or a tune

25. It's a simile, because it uses *like*.

26. **(3)** The test does not show whether he will be a good doctor, choice **(3)**. The test does show that he is good at math, choice **(1)**, and that he would be a good engineer, choice **(2)**.

27. **(1)** (paragraph 6) Choice **(2)** is not mentioned, choice **(3)** is not mentioned, and choice **(4)** is not true at the beginning of the story.

28. These are among the clues: He knows every bone in the body. He knows how all the organs connect. He wants to be a doctor with his whole heart.

29. **(4)** Vicente is in his late teens at the beginning, and he is old enough to have been in the army, established a career, gotten married, and had three children by the end.

30. **(3)** Choice **(1)** is the setting at the beginning, and choice **(2)** is the setting only in paragraph 8.

31. **(4)** All three choices are true and are mentioned in the story.

32. **(3)** The point of highest interest in the story is when Vicente, because of his knowledge about medicine, finds out what is wrong with Consuela.

33. Maybe the teachers are prejudiced against Vicente because he is Hispanic. That could be why they don't believe he could be a good doctor.

34. He thinks the illness may be all in her mind or perhaps caused by stress. The clues are his questions about whether she has had too much company or has too many children. Also, if he had taken her seriously, he wouldn't have made her wait overnight to have the tests done.

35. Vicente's conflict is with the school. It wants him to be an engineer, but he wants to be a doctor.

36. **(2)** The details of this story all add up to the statement that you must make your own decisions in life and not be influenced by what others think.

ANSWER KEY

Unit 1: Practical Reading
Chapter 1: Finding the Main Idea
Exercise 1, pages 6–7

1. how to use a microwave oven

2. how to cook broccoli for two minutes and 45 seconds at power level 5

3. You would cook green beans by pressing *2*, *3*, and *0*, then *Power,* then *7,* and finally *Start.*

4. *Start*

5. Pressing *Clear* clears the display and allows you to start again.

Exercise 2, pages 8–9

1. c

2. e

3. a

4. f

5. d

6. b

Exercise 3, pages 10–11

1. **(4)** The title and the first sentence tell you this.

2. **(2)** The second paragraph tells you how they manage.

3. **(4)** The first sentence of the paragraph is its topic sentence.

4. **(4)** Choices **(1)**, **(2)**, and **(3)** are all true.

Chapter 2: Finding Details
Exercise 1, pages 14–15

PART A

1. to advise people that some foods are better for you than others

2. grains (or bread, cereal, rice, and pasta)

3. 2 to 4 servings of fruit

4. very little

PART B

1. His body is shaped like a pyramid.

2. He is standing and eating from an open refrigerator.

Exercise 2, pages 16–17

1. Pizzarific and I Scream for Ice Cream

2. Walk forward. Go around the benches on the right and the store will be on the right.

3. Walk straight ahead around the benches on the right to the telephone area.

4. Walk straight ahead. Turn right at the bench area. Turn right again. The pizza place is the first store on his right.

Exercise 3, pages 18–19

PART A

1. k

2. f

3. n

4. b

5. h

6. j

7. a

8. i

9. d

10. e

11. m

12. g

13. l

14. c

PART B

1. d

2. e

3. b

4. c

5. a

Chapter 3: Time Order
Exercise 1, pages 22–23

1. Clean, trim, and peel the carrots.

2. Cut them into slices ½ inch thick.

3. Then put the carrots, butter, sugar, gingerroot, and chicken broth into a saucepan.

4. Simmer them, covered, for 20 minutes.

5. Then stir in the raisins.

6. Cook, uncovered, for 5 more minutes.

7. Toss the carrots with parsley.

Exercise 2, pages 24–25

1. **(2)** This detail is found in paragraph 3.

2. **(3)** This detail is found in paragraph 4.

3. **(1)** This detail is found in paragraph 3.

4. **(4)** This detail is found in paragraph 3.

5. **(2)** This detail is found in paragraph 5.

Exercise 3, pages 26–27

1. 20 minutes

2. the cool-down period

3. 140 to 160 beats per minute

4. 160 beats per minute

5. at least 5 minutes

6. 70 beats per minute

Unit 1 Review, pages 28–29

1. **(3)** The entire passage focuses on this topic. Choices **(1)** and **(4)** are supporting details. Choice **(2)** is false.

2. **(1)** Choices **(2)**, **(3)**, and **(4)** are false.

3. **(4)** Choices **(1)**, **(2)**, and **(3)** are all true.

4. **(2)** The second sentence of the paragraph tells you this detail. Choices **(1)**, **(3)**, and **(4)** are false.

5. **(2)** The third sentence of paragraph 6 gives this detail. Choices **(1)**, **(3)**, and **(4)** are false.

Unit 2: Reading Nonfiction
Chapter 4: Main Idea and Reasons
Exercise 1, pages 34–35

1. **(2)** Choices **(1)** and **(3)** are given as reasons for the main idea. Paragraph 1 implies that choice **(4)** is false.

2. **(1)** Paragraphs 2, 3, and 4 tell you why biking is booming. Choices **(2)** and **(3)** (in paragraph 5) are not true.

3. **(4)** The shortage of bike paths is discussed in paragraph 5. Choice **(1)** is given as a reason for biking (in paragraph 4), choice **(3)** (in paragraph 3) is not true, and choice **(2)** is not discussed.

4. **(3)** The fact that more riders are using helmets is mentioned in paragraph 4.

5. **(1)** The drawback of cold and icy weather in the winter months is mentioned in paragraph 5.

Exercise 2, pages 36–37

Answers may vary. Use these answers as a guideline.
1. They thought if people could read all kinds of ideas, they could decide for themselves what to think. This is discussed in paragraph 1.

2. Some people say the book is racist (paragraph 3).

3. One woman doesn't like the white people being called *demons* or the discussion of magical beings, and she thinks the book will have a bad influence on children (paragraphs 4 and 5).

4. *Dragonwings* has won awards for quality, and the school board thinks the book will help readers understand other cultures (paragraph 5).

Chapter 5: Facts and Opinions
Exercise 1, pages 40–41

1. O

2. O

3. F (The statement can be proved.)

4. F (The statement can be proved.)

5. F (The statement can be proved.)

6. O

7. O

8. F (The statement can be proved.)

9. O

10. O

Exercise 2, pages 42–43

1. **(4)** This opinion is stated in paragraphs 1 and 5.

2. **(2)** This is the only statement of the four that can be proved.

3. **(1)** This statement is a personal judgment and cannot be proved.

4. (4) This can be proved and is stated in paragraph 4.

5. (4) None of these statements can be proved.

Chapter 6: Detecting Bias
Exercise 1, pages 46–47

PART A, page 46

1. a. look, feel, and play basketball like a pro
   b. extra jumping power for slam-dunk shots
   c. for the good times in your life

2. a professional basketball player

PART B, page 47

1. a. I wouldn't be where I am today if I didn't wear Smooth Air shoes.
   b. I protect them with Smooth Airs.
   c. My feet feel comfortable.

2. (1), (5) The ad does not suggest the other choices.

Exercise 2, pages 48–49

1. T (discussed in paragraph 2)

2. F The danger of hepatitis makes it safer to use a baboon liver than a human liver for transplant (paragraph 3).

3. T (discussed in paragraph 2)

4. F (discussed in paragraph 5)

5. F (discussed in paragraph 4)

Chapter 7: Making Inferences
Exercise 1, pages 52–53

1. Statements **(1), (3), (5),** and **(6)** are either stated or shown in the cartoon.

2. Statements **(1), (3),** and **(4)** can be inferred by reading the headline.

3. Statements **(2), (4), (5),** and **(7)** can be inferred by looking at the two people in the cartoon.

4. (3) All the other choices contain opinions.

5. poorer.

Exercise 2, pages 54–55

1. S This fact is stated in the cartoon.

2. I Janis's facial expression as she says, "Yeah, yeah, I know" shows she doesn't really agree that all great chefs are men.

3. S When Janis tells Arlo how pretty his salad is, he replies "But of course!"

4. S This is shown in the third frame of the cartoon.

5. I The writer is emphasizing that men and women are not paid equally for the same work. In fact, they are given different titles.

6. S This idea is stated in the second panel of the cartoon.

7. I Arlo's self-confidence can be inferred from the first panel of the cartoon.

8. I This can be inferred because the child is asking a question about Janis and Arlo's conversation.

Unit 2 Review, pages 56–57

1. (2) This is discussed in paragraph 1.

2. (4) This is discussed in paragraph 1.

3. (3) This statement may not be true for all secretaries.

4. (1) This bias is shown throughout the article.

Unit 3: Reading Poetry
Chapter 8: Form
Exercise 1, pages 62–63

1. (4) All three choices relate to the arrangement of words in the poem that makes it look like a candy bar.

2. (3) The poet appeals to the reader's senses of sight and taste. Nothing in the poem relates to the sense of smell, hearing, or touch.

3. (2) The last three lines of the poem show how the poet feels like he's already had too much candy, but he'll have one more anyway.

4. (4) All four ingredients are mentioned in the poem.

5. (3) Snickers bars contain chocolate, peanuts, and caramel.

Exercise 2, pages 64–65

1. (4) The poet used capital letters so that the words would flow together more smoothly.

2. (3) The poet is appealing most to the sense of sight.

3. (4) The poet is having fun. He wants to entertain his readers and surprise them with his message.

Chapter 9: Rhyme and Rhythm
Exercise 1, pages 68–69

1. F The words *high* and *right* do not have the same ending. The words that do rhyme in the first verse are *strong* and *wrong, unfurled* and *world*, and *I* and *die*.

2. T Line 4 says, "I rode away to right the world."

3. F In lines 9–12, the speaker says it makes little difference if a battle is lost or won.

4. T

5. T In lines 7–8, the speaker describes good and bad as being woven in a crazy plaid, or mixed together.

6. F In lines 4–6, the speaker says she wanted to right the wrongs of the world and felt bad that she could die only once in doing so.

7. T In fact, every line is eight syllables long.

8. T The words *bad* and *plaid* (lines 7–8) rhyme, or end with the same sound.

9. (3) Now that she has aged, the speaker has learned that things usually are not all good or all bad but a mixture of both.

Exercise 2, pages 70–71

1. (1) Lines 1 and 3 rhyme, and lines 2 and 4 rhyme. Choices **(2)** and **(3)** do not have the correct rhyme pattern. Choice **(4)** is not correct because it is a rhyming poem.

2. (1) The tone of the whole poem seems romantic, but then the last line is humorous.

3. (4) Lines 7–8 speak about "the infinite, tenderest, passionate love of one dead drunk for another."

4. (2) The last line of the poem is unexpected and funny.

5. (4) *Love* is used nine times, counting the title.

Chapter 10: Imagery
Exercise 1, pages 74–75

Answers may vary. Use these answers as a guideline.

1. sight. She describes what is seen.

2. hearing. She uses the word *heard* and describes sounds.

3. Beauty can be found inside a person in the form of good deeds done and happy thoughts that repeat themselves in a person's dreams.

4. She uses the images of sunlight, trees, birds, corn growing, and people working or dancing for their harvest to show where beauty can be found.

5. nighttime

6. 3

7. The third verse has 6 lines rather than 5.

8. The last word in each verse ends with *est.*

Exercise 2, pages 76–77

1. The poet finds beauty in swallows, deer, lightning, a river, meteors, wind in the wheat, a strong-withered horse, and a runner's sure feet.

2. The poet finds beauty in the closing of the day, the pause of a wave, a crumbling ember from a fire, an opening flower, and the quiet power of an ox.

3. The poet appeals to the sense of sight in both verses.

4. Answers may vary. Use this answer as a guideline: Deer are beautiful because of the graceful way they run through the forest.

5. Answers may vary. Use this answer as a guideline: A flower that opens its petals in the wind and sways in the breeze is a beautiful sight to see.

Chapter 11: Simile and Metaphor
Exercise 1, pages 80–81

Answers may vary. Use these answers as a guideline.

1. (2) The mother's advice about not giving up is emphasized in lines 2 and 14–19. Choices **(1)**, **(3)**, and **(4)** are not shown in the text.

2. (3) Reading lines 8–13—all one sentence—could make the reader short of breath. Choice **(1)** is wrong because the line lengths are important. Choice **(2)** is wrong because the distance between mother and son is not mentioned in the poem, and choice **(4)** is not correct because the lines do not go consistently from shorter to longer length.

3. (3) Lines 3–7 and 12–13 describe a dark, dingy stairway. Choice **(1)** is not correct (see lines 2 and 20). Choice **(2)** is not correct (see lines 14–17). Choice **(4)** is not mentioned in the poem.

Answers may vary. Use these answers as a guideline.

4. Nearly the whole poem is about the mother's hard life, starting with "Life for me ain't been no crystal stair." Some other descriptive words are *splinters*, *no carpet*, and *goin' in the dark.*

5. The mother's advice is encouraging, especially "don't you turn back" and "I'se still goin', honey, I'se still climbin'."

Exercise 2, pages 82–83

1. **T** In the first verse, thoughts are compared to dead leaves. In the second verse, they are compared to fireflies.

2. **F** The comparison is not to tiredness but to dead leaves.

3. **T** Because line 4 says, "*Like* leaves . . . ," it is a simile.

4. **F** It's also a simile: "*as* thick as fireflies. . . ."

5. **T** Both *fireflies* and *shiny* have positive images.

6. **F** Both *tiredness* and *dead leaves* have negative images.

7. **F**

8. **F**

9. **T** *Inside* and *dried* rhyme.

10. **T** Lines 7–8 say, "Your thoughts as thick as fireflies/All shiny in your mind!"

Unit 3 Review, pages 84–85

1. **(2)** The squirrel's greed is discussed in lines 6–9. Choices **(1)**, **(3)**, and **(4)** are all true, but they are not main ideas.

2. **(4)** Line 5 says, "And one gray squirrel named Joe."

3. **(1)** The difference in line lengths adds interest to the poem. Choices **(2)**, **(3)**, and **(4)** are all untrue.

4. **(3)** *Snow* and *Joe* (lines 2 and 5) rhyme, and *seeds* and *breeds* (lines 3 and 4) rhyme.

5. **(3)** *Late* and *wait* (lines 7 and 9) rhyme, and *go* and *snow* (lines 10 and 11) rhyme.

6. **(4)** Choices **(1)**, **(2)**, and **(3)** are all images described in the poem.

7. **(1)** The fact that the squirrel is a bully is hinted at in lines 6–9. Choices **(2)**, **(3)**, and **(4)** are not shown in the text.

8. **(3)** Line 1 mentions winter; lines 2 and 11 mention snow.

Unit 4: Reading Short Fiction
Chapter 12: Character
Exercise, pages 90–95

1. **(4)** The four characters named in the story are Joey, Frank, Mr. Lovides, and Ralph. Frank's wife, the minister, and the new man working the second counter are such minor characters that they are not named.

2. **(1)** Joey finds Mr. Lovides frightening until the last three paragraphs.

3. **(3)** Choices **(1)** and **(4)** are wrong because Joey realizes he's *not* cruel or prejudiced. Choice **(2)** is not mentioned anywhere in the story.

4. **(4)** Frank says in paragraph 3 that Mr. Lovides's eyes are gentle and compassionate.

5. **(1)** Frank's behavior toward Joey shows him to be warm and friendly. Choices **(2)**, **(3)**, and **(4)** are not supported by the story.

6. **(3)** Paragraphs 8 and 13 state that Joey likes sharp, dressy clothes.

7. **(2)** The story says that Joey gains confidence and pride.

8. **(4)** Choices **(1)** and **(3)** are shown throughout the story, especially in paragraph 16. Choice **(2)** is mentioned in paragraphs 13 and 23.

9. **(1)** Having long black eyelashes describes Joey, not Frank (paragraph 16). Choices **(2)**, **(3)**, and **(4)** describe Frank (paragraph 14).

10. **(3)** New York City; the words in the story suggest a large metropolitan area.

Answers may vary. Use these answers as a guideline.

11. (a) hiring Joey as second counterman when Ralph quits, (b) allowing Joey to attend Frank's wedding, (c) not criticizing Joey for being rude to one customer, and (d) promoting Joey to first counterman.

12. Joey's way of talking suggests that he is new to the country: "Frank said he speak to you, ask you to let me off for his marriage. To be witness."

Chapter 13: Setting
Exercise, pages 98–103

1. Paragraph 15 says that the story takes place in late summer.

2. It is set in a real place. (See answer 3.)

3. It takes place in the Dominican Republic, not the United States. Clues are the kind of money mentioned in paragraph 15 (Dominican peso), paragraph 43 (ten-peso coin), and the presence of American tourists.

4. Among the clues are (a) rustling palm trees, (b) shade under a palm tree, (c) baskets of mangoes and oranges, (d) "It was too hot for the lady . . . ," and (e) a thick breeze.

5. Among the clues are these: (a) They live in a bark-walled house; their living conditions are poor. (b) The children must sell fruit to help the family survive. (c) Miguel must do chores for tourists so he can earn money. (d) The family keeps a goat and raises chickens for food. (e) The twenty-dollar bill means wealth to them. (f) They have no running water. (g) Juana can't afford to send her children to school.

6. No. Paragraph 21 says the American woman couldn't understand him.

7. Clues that one of the children is sick are: (a) The smallest child is listless (paragraph 6) and whimpers and coughs (paragraph 48). (b) The twenty dollars will be used to buy medicine (paragraph 47).

8. No. She waited until he was asleep to give the $20 to Miguel (paragraphs 39–42).

9. It costs too much money (paragraphs 46 and 52).

10.

	Carreras family	American tourists
beach	rocky, dangerous	smooth, soft, sandy, safe
housing	bark-walled house, leaky roof, smell of sewage, dump, foul stream	pink hotel
ways each spends time	working: hauling water, washing clothes, taking care of younger children and animals	playing: fishing, swimming, parasailing, sunbathing
food	rice, goat milk, eggs, chicken	pizza, Coke

Chapter 14: Plot
Exercise, pages 106–111

PART A

The order of events in the story is 5, 1, 2, 4, 6, 3.

PART B

1. (2) "The guy" is the first character introduced in the story. Choices (1) and (3) are introduced later. Choice (4) is not in the story.

2. (1) This is the central conflict of the story. Choice (3) is not true because Howard is almost able to keep up with the younger man. Choices (2) and (4) are not important to the story.

3. (3) Choice (3) is the only conclusion Howard leaps to.

4. (2) This is shown when the young man throws his wallet back at Howard and keeps running.

5. (4) In this story, the climax comes in the very last paragraph.

6. **(4)** The story starts out on a subway train, then moves to city streets, then back to the train, and then to Howard's office.

7. **(3)** This is shown in paragraph 10 as he eyes every passenger suspiciously.

8. **(4)** This description is given in paragraphs 2 and 6.

9. **(3)** This is mentioned in paragraph 4, though the man is described in more detail in paragraph 1.

10. Answers may vary. Use this answer as a guideline: Yes, the ending is effective. It surprises the reader and drives home the theme that people often jump to wrong conclusions about people who are different from them.

Chapter 15: Conflict
Exercise, pages 114–117

PART A

1. She sees his neck brace and thinks he may have been injured in their car accident. She worries that Hank may sue her.

2. From the mention of her downstairs neighbor (paragraph 5), you know she lives in an apartment building.

3. They are Hank and Elly's infant daughters. If the narrator tells Elly about her affair with Hank, Elly and Hank may break up and their daughters will be affected.

4. Hank is a fire fighter. He rescued the narrator and her neighbors from a burning building.

5. The narrator wants to tell Hank's wife that she is in love with her husband and can't wait until the twins grow up to be with him.

PART B

1. **(3)** Choices **(1)**, **(2)**, and **(4)** are all true, but they are not the central conflict of the story.

2. **(1)** Choice **(2)** is true, but it is an external conflict. Choice **(3)** is not mentioned, and choice **(4)** is clearly untrue.

3. **(2)** The other three choices are not mentioned in the story.

4. **(1)** The narrator's blue eyes are mentioned in paragraph 8.

5. **(4)** The narrator is confused. She is driving around trying to decide if she should call Hank's wife and meet with her. She thought she could just flirt with Elly's husband without bad consequences, "but now a thing has happened," and she "can't wait."

6. **(3)** The narrator is driving around the Henkinses' neighborhood trying to work up enough courage to call Elly and go to talk to Elly (paragraph 9).

Chapter 16: Theme and Main Idea
Exercise, pages 120–123

PART A

1. **T** Noni has had nothing to eat for three days and will soon starve if he doesn't eat his dog.

2. **F** Even though Nimuk is starving too, he refuses to hurt Noni.

3. **F** He sharpens an iron strip into a knife to use for killing Nimuk.

4. **T** In the last four paragraphs, the glint of sun on the knife is what tells the pilot that someone is on the ice floe.

5. **F** In fact, the outcome of this story contradicts that theme.

6. **T** This is shown in how Nimuk and Noni treat one another in spite of almost starving to death.

7. **T** He wants to live, but he doesn't want to hurt Nimuk.

8. **F** In fact, the pilot is the person who rescues Nimuk and Noni.

9. **T** Hunger and freezing cold are what threaten his life.

10. **F** The setting is an Arctic ice floe, probably in Alaska or Canada.

11. **F** The story takes place since airplane flight became common, or within the last 50 years or so.

12. **T** He risks his life for his dog.

13. **F** Noni is shown as selfless and loving.

14. **F** Nimuk wants affection more than food, even though he's starving.

15. **T** Even if one had eaten the other, the survivor eventually would have starved.

PART B

Answers may vary. Use these answers as a guideline.

1. Noni shows compassion first, when he throws away the knife he made to use for killing Nimuk (paragraph 17).

2. Usually, animals attack humans. But Noni decides he will starve if he doesn't eat the dog, while the dog would rather take comfort in the boy Noni's nearness than eat him to survive.

3. Noni thinks Nimuk is going to attack him. Instead, he licks the boy's face.

4. The pilot sees sunlight glinting on the homemade knife Noni threw away and decides to come down for a closer look (paragraphs 24–27).

5. Noni does not want to remember that the reason he is making the knife is to use it to kill his dog and eat him so he can survive.

Unit 4 Review, pages 124–129

1. **(4)** Her age (sixteen) is stated in paragraph 17. The fact that she wants to be a writer is in paragraph 43, and her homesickness is emphasized throughout the story.

2. **(2)** Her father does not like the city and is not running away from his family. Choice **(3)**, that he paints portraits and is looking for new subjects, is true of Beth, not the father.

3. **(1)** Paragraph 15 states that the main character thinks Beth laughs and cries a lot. Choices **(2)** and **(3)**, that she's very old and not friendly, are not true. Choice **(4)**, that she hates city life, is not mentioned.

4. **(3)** The narrator dreams of choices **(1)** and **(4)**, the mountains of Appalachia and her high school classroom, and her father dreams of the Kentucky Blue Grass country, choice **(2)**, but the story is set in a drugstore snack counter in Chicago.

5. **(2)** The climax is when the main character quits her job. Choice **(1)** is an event that helps build suspense, choice **(3)** is the conclusion, and choice **(4)** is not one event but rather a constant background.

6. **(4)** The main character has an external conflict with Ellen. She gets along well with her father, choice **(1)**, and her mother, choice **(2)**, and no conflict is shown with Beth, choice **(3)**.

7. **(1)** The main character's internal conflict is that she wants to be back home but has to earn money. Choices **(3)** and **(4)** are not true. Choice **(2)** is not presented as a conflict.

8. **(2)** Choice **(3)** is not true, choice **(1)** is not the main point of the story, and choice **(4)** is not a point of the story.

9. **(3)** This is reinforced when the narrator says (paragraph 39), "Artist. Any artist. That word is magic. . . . This woman is not a *person*-person like the bodies in the streets. This woman stands for big places—mystery places. Moving on."

10. **(4)** The main characters of "Appalachian Home" and "The Eyes of Mr. Lovides" work in a diner, have moved to a different place, and are often lonely and uncomfortable.

11. **(3)** The main character is different from Joey because she decides to go home. Choices **(1)** and **(2)** are not true because it is Joey who is from Puerto Rico and apparently all alone in the world. Choice **(4)** is not true of the main character in this story.